WESLEY SPEAKS ON CHRISTIAN VOCATION

Paul Wesley Chilcote

Foreword by David L. Watson

DISCIPLESHIP RESOURCES
MATERIALS FOR GROWTH IN CHRISTIAN FAITH AND LIFE
P.O. Box 840 • Nashville, TN 37202 • Phone (615) 340-7068

ISBN 0-88177-041-8

Library of Congress Catalog Card No. 86-72686

CONTENTS

CHAPTER 3. HOW TO TEACH

CHAPTER 4. WHAT TO DO

FOREWORD

Methodism as a church has always had something of a double identity. On the one hand, its members have been strongly committed to Christian discipleship, and have yearned for the personal walk with Christ which sustains them in this task. Yet there has also been the necessity of nurturing and sustaining an institutional church, which time and again has seemed to distract from the more immediate call to witness and service in the world.

Most especially has this been true of Methodists in North America. As the Bicentennial of the Christmas Conference of 1784 reminded us, the Methodist Episcopal Church was the mother church of world Methodism. As a movement, the early Methodist societies, classes and bands, had been a vital force in popular religion on both sides of the Atlantic. But in declaring themselves to be a church, North American Methodists took a step which rendered them an integral part of the structure as well as the spirit of the religious life of their nation.

They have wrestled with this identity for more than two hundred years, and the struggle has not been easy. On the one hand, they were quickly caught up in the Second Great Awakening of the early nineteenth century, which profoundly affected their understanding of the gospel, and which ill prepared them to withstand the folk religiosity of frontier evangelism. On the other hand, their polity as a church was forged in the very mixed climate of a political revolution, the implications of which were not immediately clear to their founder and mentor in England.

Wesley himself was always a churchman, convinced of the validity and necessity of the visible church, with its doctrine, discipline, and means of grace. Yet his life's work was to proclaim a gospel of salvation, at the heart of which was a call to discipleship generated and sustained by a relationship with Jesus Christ. It was one thing to provide a connectional network for Methodist societies in which this discipleship could be nurtured within the Church of England. But making the transition to an institutional church required North American Methodists to establish, albeit with Wesley's guidance, their own doctrine, discipline, and polity. This did not, and has not, come easily to those whose faith has always been oriented to personal and social witness. As a result, the double identity of churchly Methodism has sometimes become split.

The irony in all of this is that the wisdom of Wesley himself has in large measure been ignored. His understanding of the gospel, when it has been retained at the center of Methodist teaching (and this more often than not in the separatist Methodist churches), has provided a strong corrective to personalized folk religion. Where his understanding of the visible church has prevailed, there has likewise been an anchor to which the victims of fractious groupings have returned time and again. In a word, Wesley's discipleship was Christ-centered and church-centered both, and for the best of reasons: This is the way Jesus told us to get on with the job.

In the pages which follow, Paul Chilcote has culled from the writings of Wesley some very fine passages, many of them real nuggets, which confirm precisely such understandings. Christian discipleship emerges, not as a personal amphetamine, nor yet as a social panacea, but as a responsible, methodical, churchly response to a call from the risen Jew of Nazareth.

As one of the new generation of Wesley scholars, Dr. Chilcote's research is exemplary. But more, his selections and his introductions tell us that he stands in the most significant lineage of all: the evangelical tradition of those who have directly received from Christ their call to discipleship. It was this which Wesley discerned when he first described Methodists as those who, having the form, sought the power of godliness. Without neglecting for one moment the propriety of the form, Paul Chilcote points us to the source of the power.

These selections should be read, over and over again. They are the very stuff of Methodism.

DAVID LOWES WATSON

PROLOGUE

On the last day of Vacation Church School, a little third-grader popped into my study to say, "Good morning." I asked her if she was going to be in church on Sunday for our big celebration. Somewhat puzzled by my question, she immediately replied: "Of course I'll be there! I'm baptized!" On Sunday morning, there she was in her usual place, with three neighborhood children she had invited to share her joy.

That little girl had a very clear understanding of who she was and to whom she belonged. No one could have illustrated Christ's promise to all and his claim upon his own more dramatically. In baptism she received a precious gift and assumed a challenging responsibility. She was in ministry. She was living out her true vocation as a member of Christ's Body. She had translated her experience of being loved and accepted into action. Empowered by God's grace, she was an agent for renewal, helping to make the community of God's new covenant a reality for others.

Christian vocation means calling. Christian vocation is our calling to new life in Christ. Christ calls us to become learners ("disciples") and gathers us into a pilgrim community to teach us how to love. Then he sends us out ("apostles") to serve the present age by sharing that love with others. We are called, not because of what we have done but because we are God's own people, formed by God's purpose and grace.

To be faithful witnesses in our own time we must ask penetrating questions about our life in Christ and our life together.

- Where can I see Christ at work in my life? our community? the world?
- What is Christ calling me to be and to do?
- How can peace and justice and love be experienced as realities in my own life and that of my family?
- What does it mean to be a part of the family of God?
- What is my vocation as a Christian in pilgrimage with other persons committed to Christ and his way?

These perennial questions are personal and intimate. They involve a process of discernment which always moves us from believing to doing, from contemplation to action. These questions and this process help us to identify the primary issues surrounding our vocation in Christ today. The amazing legacy of faith working by love, which we have inherited from a great cloud of witnesses, is a rich resource to apply to this task. Our pilgrimage of faith is greatly enhanced as we draw upon the accumulated wisdom of the past.

The original questions posed by John Wesley at the Methodist conference of 1744 provide a natural and appropriate framework for the rediscovery of our ministry and mission in the world today.

- What do we teach?
- How do we teach?
- What do we do?

These questions strike at the heart of our quest. In his lifelong response to these questions, Wesley addressed many of the vocational issues we face in our own time. Is it possible to achieve a healthy balance of evangelical experience and social service? What resources are available to those who minister to the complex needs of others and can be easily "burned out" in the process? What is the appropriate response of Christians to a world that is hungry and torn apart by war? The issues are bluntly contemporary. Wesley's responses to them are challenging.

The material which follows, therefore, has been compiled from the writings of John (and Charles) Wesley for purposes of study and reflection, either by individuals or within the context of small groups. Each chapter is divided into three basic parts: A. Introduction; B. Wesley Speaks; C. For Thought and Discussion.

A brief essay focuses the vocational theme in its contemporary perspective and introduces the Wesley material as a resource. These resources include a variety of pertinent selections from Wesley's wide-ranging corpus. A sampling of succinct statements or excerpts from letters, sermons, treatises, or hymns, which opens each Wesley Speaks section, illustrates his understanding of the issues related to Christian vocation. In addition, a number of Wesley's published sermons and tracts, reproduced in modernized and abridged form, expand the themes and provide an opportunity to explore the wider dimensions of discipleship in the Wesleyan tradition. Finally, focused questions have been provided to stimulate thought, discussion, or action concerning the application of Wesleyan vocational principles to your life today.

Individual Use

How can this resource be used? If you are using this book primarily as a personal manual, let me suggest several directions. The material lends itself very well to a retreat setting. An overnight program of spiritual formation at a retreat center could prove to be a very meaningful experience. Here is a suggested program of study/reflection:

DAY ONE   10:00 A.M.   Read Chapter 1
                                       Begin Journal Writing
              12:00 noon   Lunch
                1:00 P.M.   Read Chapter 2
                                         Meditation/Quiet Reflection
                                         Journal Writing
                4:00 P.M.   Sacrificial Meal
                5:00 P.M.   Read Chapter 3
                                         Meditation/Quiet Reflection
                                         Journal Writing

DAY TWO   7:00 A.M.   Breakfast
               8:00 A.M.   Read Chapter 4
                                       Meditation/Quiet Reflection
                                         Journal Writing
                                         Read Epilogue
             11:30 A.M.   Read/Celebrate Service of
                                       Covenant Renewal in
                                       Book of Worship

Journal writing is mentioned in this suggested outline. Some participants might find it helpful to keep a record of thoughts and impressions throughout the course of this study. Journal writing is an important part of the Methodist legacy which is being rediscovered today. A renewed emphasis upon spiritual formation within the church has drawn attention to this practice as a significant means of grace. The questions at the conclusion of each chapter may be used as a guide for thoughtful written reflection as well as for purposes of discussion within groups.

Some readers may choose to study these materials devotionally throughout the course of a week. Others may prefer to stretch the reading out over the period of a month with a designated time for study each week.

The preparatory seasons of the Christian Year are particularly suited for this kind of reflection. The four-week Advent season prior to Christmas and the five-week period in Lent prior to Palm/Passion Sunday are ideal. The lengthy season following Pentecost is an appropriate time to reflect upon the church's mission in the world.

Group Use

Small groups may also find these basic suggestions helpful. A prototype of this study, originally designed as a resource for clergy in the North Indiana Conference, formed the basis of discussion for cluster groups meeting weekly or semi-weekly over the course of six to eight weeks. Groups such as these, with approximately four to seven members, correspond to the band-meetings of early Methodism. Leadership in such groups can be shared by the participants; or a specific leader may be chosen by the group to guide them through the study.

Pastors may wish to identify persons in their congregations who are earnestly seeking to explore their pilgrimage with Christ more deeply. This study could be used effectively, therefore, in church school classes, special study series, or in ongoing Bible studies. A small group composed of area pastors and lay leaders could afford some exciting opportunities for growth, fellowship, and service. The book may also be used as a tool to help councils on ministry/administrative councils discover important areas of ministry and service in their communities.

The study might be used by those members of local congregations who are earnestly seeking to explore their pilgrimage with Christ more deeply. The early Methodists did this through a weekly *class meeting,* where they gathered to give an account to each other of their discipleship during the past week. Their guidelines were Wesley's *General Rules,* which fell into two broad categories: "works of mercy"—how to serve, and how not to sin against, God and one's neighbor; and "works of piety" or "means of grace"—worship, sacrament, prayer, Bible study, fellowship, and fasting. These guidelines appear time and again in the selections which follow, and they were clearly designed to nurture and strengthen the discipleship of the early Methodists.

Today, an increasing number of congregations are forming Covenant Discipleship Groups,[1] patterned after the early class meeting, and with

[1]For information on Covenant Discipleship Groups, write to: The General Board of Discipleship, P.O. Box 840, Nashville, TN 37202. See also David Lowes Watson, *Accountable Discipleship* (Nashville: Discipleship Resources, Revised 1986. Cat. # DR009B.)

the same purpose. Wesley's writings can be a guide for their discipleship today no less than for the early Methodists, and this study is commended to them as a further insight into their Methodist heritage.

Many Christians who stand outside the Wesleyan tradition are discovering Wesley for the first time. For them, he has become a significant mentor in the faith. When shared with members of other faith communities, this book may lead to some startling affirmations of our unity in Christ.

This book is for committed Christians, lay and clergy, who want to recapture the vitality of being in ministry. It is particularly directed toward those who want to explore the meaning of discipleship in greater depth and from a Wesleyan perspective. It is for people who want to explore concrete issues surrounding Christian witness and service in our world today. This book is for those who are serious about the need for all of Christ's disciples to be engaged in a ministry of reconciliation for the world. Together, we need to discern the movement of God's Spirit in our age. If we are sensitive and open, God will enable us to grow in Christian love and holiness. God will empower us to be faithful as a witnessing and serving community.

> Christ, whose glory fills the skies,
>   Christ, the true, the only light,
> Sun of Righteousness, arise,
>   Triumph o'er the shades of night;
> Day-spring from on high, be near,
> Day-star, in my heart appear.
>
> Dark and cheerless is the morn
>   Unaccompanied by Thee:
> Joyless is the day's return,
>   Till Thy mercy's beams I see,
> Till Thou inward light impart,
> Glad my eyes, and warm my heart.
>
> Visit then this soul of mine;
>   Pierce the gloom of sin and grief;
> Fill me, Radiancy divine;
>   Scatter all my unbelief;
> More and more Thyself display,
> Shining to the perfect day.[2]

[2] Originally published in *Hymns and Sacred Poems* (London: Strahan, 1740).

CHAPTER 1
THE WESLEYAN REDISCOVERY
OF CHRISTIAN VOCATION

A. Introduction

John Wesley was a pilgrim and an explorer. He lived as though a life of gratitude was itself the greatest act of devotion. His spiritual journey was a quest for the fullness of God's love expressed in sacrificial love for others.

Wesley was not alone in this pilgrimage of faith. He shared the journey with a host of faithful companions. Following in the footsteps of Paul, Augustine, Francis, and Luther, he pressed on toward the high goal to love God and neighbor. His story is captivating because it mirrors your story and mine.

Archbishop William Temple once described the essence of the Christian faith as an experience of the love of God in Christ changing our hopes and desires. No definition could better characterize Wesley's life. The foundation upon which he built his life and his movement was a personal relationship with the living Lord. He believed that this gift was a transforming friendship available to all. He discovered the freedom of living in the grace of God, and that discovery changed his life and his world.

Today, in an era of constant and monumental change, what forces shape our hopes and desires? All of us feel the pain of our wounds and the impotence of struggling discipleship. One day an anguished colleague said to me, "I feel so isolated! We're lost without each other, but we never have any opportunity to share our dreams and failures." The committed lay person asks, "In the face of our world's problems, what can one person do? How can I put my gifts to work in the service of Christ?"

No better mentor could be found in this quest than John Wesley. In an era not unlike our own, he redirected people to the proper foundation of a life of faith. He helped them to discover that a sojourn through life with

1

Christ is the greatest adventure of all. He provided means to nurture and empower his fellow pilgrims. Many of his discoveries can bring new life and excitement into your spiritual journey today.

Wesley rediscovered the Bible as a place of divine encounter where the living Word can be met and known. Dead words became the Word of Life to countless disciples. Living faith nurtured in fellowship was the Methodist staff of life. Classic spiritual disciplines supported, nourished, and guided them on their way. Mutual accountability not only guarded them from dangerous diversions, but strengthened the pastoral gifts of faithful lay pioneers.

In all of this, Wesley's primary concern was for the realization of God's dream in every person. Wherever he saw truth, he embraced it. He enabled his followers to discover their hidden potential and to fulfill their vocation as the children of God. By allowing his co-workers to grow in grace, he empowered them for ministry. His quest was for Christian wholeness; his driving passion was to bring balance and vitality to the Christian life.

VOCATION DEFINED

Christian vocation, then, if it is to be true to the Wesleyan spirit, must be rooted in the transforming experience of God's grace manifest in Jesus Christ and realized through the power of the Holy Spirit. This is where our journey must begin.

If we take this preliminary description of Christian vocation as our starting point, then several fundamental issues emerge. First of all, vocation must be understood as a *gift* to which the only appropriate response is doxology, that is, a life of unceasing prayer and praise. Second, vocation is a *calling* which reorients and radically transforms the lives of those who respond in faith. And third, while vocation is necessarily an intensely personal matter, it can only be realized fully as it is lived out in *community*.

Gift. Most of us have been raised on a steady diet of rugged individualism. Our tendency is to emphasize or value human potential and achievement rather than divine initiative. But Christian vocation, like faith itself, is a gift. The whole process of discovering, and nurturing, and fulfilling our vocation in Christ is a matter of grace. Vocation is not something we can hope to create; rather, it is a gift which God empowers us both to receive and to perfect. All of life, when lived vocationally in Christ, is prayer.

Call. The vocation of every Christian, therefore, is experienced initially as a call. It is a call not simply to believe, but to follow; it is an invitation not merely to be a "believer," but to become a "disciple." Many churches today are filled with "members" who have never discovered the challenge and joy of "discipleship." Their true vocation is a call, a summons to enter a particular, revolutionary path of self-sacrificing love for the world. God's call in Christ Jesus is an invitation to participate in a new age of peace with justice, founded upon the reckless abandonment of power and self.

Community. This kind of abandonment is embraced by and embraces what appears to be foolishness in the eyes of the world. And so, those who believe are not only called out of darkness and death, but into fellowship with a crucified Lord, into a communion of martyrs (literally witnesses) of the faith, and into a freedom that is bondage to love. Nowhere is the corporate nature of our vocation more visible than in our solidarity with the least, and the last, and the lost of the world.

Wesley offers profound insights in each of these areas. He believed that Christian life is devotion. The classics of Christian spirituality taught him the importance of total consecration in the love of God and neighbor. He recognized the necessity of community in the development of a balanced program of spiritual formation. His "way of devotion" was one of personal encounter with Christ plus shared Christian experience.

In the selections on the way of devotion that follow, pay close attention to the centrality of prayer in the Christian life. But note also Wesley's recurring insistence upon the corporate nature of Christian vocation. For him, vocation, in all of its dimensions, concerns the way in which the life of prayer influences our conduct, our style of life, and our attitudes toward other people. Prayer, both in its private forms and as an expression of the worshiping Body of Christ, shapes belief, inspires movements, and builds community.

"The Almost Christian," a sermon which Wesley preached at Oxford University, stands as the second of his so-called "standard sermons." When he ascended the pulpit of St. Mary's Church on July 25, 1741 to preach this controversial sermon, the evangelical revival under his direction was a fresh movement of great proportions. The central theme of this manifesto is the radical difference between nominal and real Christianity—between those who believe and those who have become disciples of Christ. In an effort to stress the urgency of transformation in life, he contrasts the "almost" Christian with the person who is "altogether"

Christian by grace. Consider the nature of your own experience and commitment as you reflect upon these two stages of growth in Christ.

Wesley's sermon "On God's Vineyard" was published in 1788. In this sermonic-essay, the aged evangelist attempts to assess the Methodist revival after fifty years. The sermon recalls the origins and essentials of a powerful religious awakening. As in all of Wesley's sermons (his published sermons are really essays in which a particular theme is formally addressed) the focus is on application. From the extemporaneous orations in the fields and industrial centers of Britain to the experimental statements on living vocation expressed in his published sermons, Wesley's intention was patently personal and practical. His insights can help you to project a path for your own ministry as you discern God's guidance in this time and this place.

B. Wesley Speaks

1. SELECTIONS ON THE WAY OF DEVOTION

A Life of Devotion

I take religion to be . . . a constant ruling habit of soul, a renewal of our minds in the image of God, a recovery of the Divine likeness, a still-increasing conformity of heart and life to the pattern of our most holy Redeemer.

(In a letter to Richard Morgan, dated 1734)

I resolved to dedicate all my life to God, all my thoughts and words and actions, being thoroughly convinced there was no medium, but that every part of my life (not some only) must either be a sacrifice to God, or to myself; that is, in effect, to the devil. . . . I determined, through his grace (the absolute necessity of which I was deeply sensible of) to be all-devoted to God.

(In "A Plain Account of Christian Perfection," 1777. Wesley refers here to his "religious conversion" of 1725 which immediately preceded his ordination to the priesthood.)

Oh what a thing it is to have *curam animarum* [the cure of souls]! You and I are called to this; to save souls from death; to watch over them as those that must give account! If our office implied no more than preaching a few times in a week, I could play with it; so might you. But how small a part of our duty (yours as well as mine) is this! God says to you, as well as me, "Do all thou canst, be it more or less, to save the souls for whom my Son has died."

(In a letter to Charles Wesley, dated March 25, 1772)

Give me one hundred preachers who fear nothing but sin and desire nothing but God, and I care not a straw whether they be clergymen or laymen, such alone will shake the gates of hell and set up the kingdom of Heaven on earth.

(In a letter to Alexander Mather, dated 1777)

Private Devotions

O begin! Fix some part of every day for private exercises. . . . Whether you like it or no, read and pray daily. It is for your life; there is no other way: else you will be a trifler all your days.

(In a letter to a would-be Methodist)

On every occasion of uneasiness we should retire to prayer, that we may give place to the grace and light of God. . . . Prayer continues in the desire of the heart, though the understanding is employed on outward things.

(In "A Plain Account of Christian Perfection," 1777)

Perhaps no sin of omission more frequently occasions (dullness of spirit) than the neglect of private prayer; the want whereof cannot be supplied by any other ordinance whatever. Nothing can be more plain, than that the life of God in the soul does not continue, much less increase, unless we use all opportunities of communion with God, and pouring out our hearts before him. If, therefore, we are negligent of this, . . . life will surely decay.

(In "The Wilderness State," 1760)

Christian Fellowship

Who watched over [the parishioners] in love? Who marked their growth in grace? Who advised and exhorted them from time to time? Who prayed

with them and for them, as they had need? This, and this alone is
Christian fellowship: But, alas, where is it to be found? Look east or west,
north or south; name what parish you please: Is this Christian fellowship
there? Rather, are not the bulk of parishioners a mere rope of sand? What
Christian connection is there between them? What intercourse in spiritual things? What watching over each other's souls? What bearing of one
another's burdens? . . . We introduce fellowship where it was utterly destroyed. And the fruits of it have been peace, joy, love, and zeal for every
good word and work.

> *(In "The People Called Methodists," 1748)*

A society is no other than a company of men [and women] having the
form and seeking the power of godliness, united in order to pray together,
to receive the word of exhortation, and to watch over one another in love,
that they may help each other to work out their salvation.

> *(In "The Rules of the United Societies," 1743. The small*
> *groups of men and women that formed around Wesley*
> *in order to bring renewal to the Church of England*
> *were originally known as "societies." They functioned*
> *as ecclesiolae in ecclesia [little churches within the*
> *church], seeking revitalization from within.)*

It is only when we are knit together that we "have nourishment from
Him, and increase with the increase of God." Neither is there any time,
when the weakest member can say to the strongest, or the strongest to
the weakest, "I have no need of thee." Accordingly our blessed Lord, when
his disciples were in the weakest state, sent them forth, not alone, but
two by two. When they were strengthened a little, not by solitude, but by
abiding with him and one another, he commanded them to "wait," not
separate, but "being assembled together," for "the promise of the Father."

> *(In "Notes on the New Testament," 1755)*

I was more convinced than ever, that the preaching like an apostle,
without joining together those that are awakened, and training them up
in the ways of God, is only begetting children for the murderer.

> *(In the Journal, dated August 25, 1763)*

After some time spent in prayer, the design of our meeting was
proposed, namely, to consider,

1. What to teach;
2. How to teach; and

3. What to do, i.e., how to regulate our doctrine, discipline and practice.

> *(In "The Minutes of the Conference," 1744. These were the questions addressed to the first Methodist Conference meeting in London in that year.)*

2. THE ALMOST CHRISTIAN

You almost persuade me to be a Christian.

(Acts 26:28)

1. Ever since the coming of Christ into the world, there have been many in every age and nation who were "almost persuaded to be Christians." How important it is for each of us to consider, however, what is implied in being *almost* a Christian, and what it means to be *altogether* a Christian.

Characteristics of the Almost Christian

2. Those who are almost Christian may be characterized, first of all, by their *honesty*. They obey the rules that are commonly expected of one another. They are not unjust. They do not steal from their neighbors. They do not oppress the poor. Indeed, there is a sort of love and assistance which they expect from one another. And this may even extend into their feeding of the hungry if they have food to spare, clothing the naked with their own superfluous clothing, and giving to any that are in need so long as they do not have need themselves.

3. A second thing implied in being almost a Christian is having *a form of godliness*—having the outside of a real Christian. They obey the ten commandments. The almost Christian may even go beyond the letter of the law in doing good to others. They reprove the wicked, instruct the ignorant, confirm the wavering, encourage the good, and comfort those who are afflicted in any way.

4. Those who have the form of godliness also use the means of grace. They attend worship regularly. They are serious and attentive in every part of the worship service. Whenever they receive the Lord's Supper, everything in their behavior would seem to speak: "God, be merciful to me, a

sinner!" They have daily prayers in their homes, and they set special times aside for devotions and meditation on the things of God.

5. In addition to all of this, the almost Christian is also *sincere*. By sincerity I mean a real, inward principle of religion out of which these actions flow. The almost Christian is not moved to any of these actions by the fear of being punished, but truly desires to follow God. There is a real design to serve God, a hearty desire to do God's will. And this motive runs through the whole tenor of life. It is the moving principle for doing good, abstaining from evil, and using the ordinance of God.

6. I speak to you all very boldly. And I do so because this was the tenor of my life for many years as many of you know. I avoided all evil in order to have a clear conscience. I used every opportunity I had to do good to everyone. I was devout both in public and private prayer, in the study of scripture, and in receiving Holy Communion. And God is my record, before whom I stand; I did all of this in sincerity. My design was to serve God, to do God's will in all things, to please God who had called me to "fight the good fight," and to "win eternal life for myself." Yet in all of this, I was but *almost a Christian.*

The Altogether Christian

7. The first thing implied in being altogether a Christian is *the love of God*. The Bible says: "Love the Lord your God with all your heart, with all your soul, with all your mind, and with all your strength." This kind of love captures the whole heart, takes up all the affections, fills the entire capacity of the soul, and uses every gift to its fullest extent. The heart of this disciple continually cries out, "My Lord and my God." "What else do I have in heaven but you? Since I have you, what else could I want on earth?"

8. The second thing implied in being altogether a Christian is the *love of our neighbor.* For our Lord says: "Love your neighbor as you love yourself." And if anyone asks, Who is my neighbor? we reply, "Every person who is in the world; every child of God." Neither can we exclude our enemies or the enemies of God and their own souls. But every Christian loves these as Christ has loved us. Whoever would more fully understand what kind of love this is may consider St. Paul's description of it in 1 Corinthians 13.

9. One thing remains to be considered, namely, the foundation of these dual loves of God and neighbor. The ground of all—what makes this kind

of love possible—is *faith*. Faith is the keynote of scripture. "Whoever believes that Jesus is the Messiah," says the beloved disciple, "is a child of God." He goes on to say that "we win the victory over the world by means of faith." Jesus himself declares, "whoever believes in him may not die but have eternal life," indeed, "has already passed from death to life."

10. But do not be deceived. The faith of which our Lord speaks is a "living faith." It is a faith that works by love. "The right and true Christian faith is" (to go on in the words of our own Church) "not only to believe that Holy Scripture and the articles of our faith are true, but also to have a sure trust and confidence to be saved from everlasting damnation by Christ."[3] Faith is a "sure trust and confidence" that Christ [died for *me* and saved *me* from the law of sin and death].

11. This faith purifies the heart by the power of God who dwells therein. It fills the heart with love stronger than death—a love both to God and to all humankind. Whoever has received this love, rejoices in spending their whole life for others. Whoever has this faith which works by love is not *almost* only, but *altogether* a Christian.

A Practical Application

12. But who are the living witnesses of these things? I pray that each of you would ask in the depths of your heart: "Am I of that number? Am I just, merciful, and honest? If so, do I have the *outside* of a Christian? The form of godliness? Do I avoid evil, pursue good, use all of the means of grace God affords me? And do I have a sincere desire to please God in all of this?

13. Perhaps you have not even come this far. Perhaps you are not even *almost* a Christian? But if you have, do good designs and sincerity make a Christian? Someone has said that "the way to hell is paved with good intentions." The greatest question of all still remains: Is the love of God shed abroad in your heart? Can you cry out, "My Lord and my all?" Do you desire nothing but God? Are you happy in God? Is God your glory, your delight, your crown of rejoicing?

---

[3]Wesley refers here to one of the "Homilies" of the Church of England dealing with "the Salvation of Man." The *Book of Homilies* was a collection of sermons addressing critical theological and ethical concerns. Compiled during the period of the English Reformation in the sixteenth century, this rich resource attained a certain status of authority within the Church of England. Wesley abridged portions of it for his own use and drew upon it frequently in his discussion of doctrinal matters.

14. And is this commandment written on your heart: "Whoever loves God must love his brother also?" Do you love your neighbor as yourself? Do you love every person, even your enemies, even the enemies of God, as your own soul? As Christ loved you? Do you believe that Christ died for *you,* and gave himself for you? Do you believe that the Lamb of God has taken away *your* sins? Does the Spirit bear witness with *your* spirit that you are a child of God?

15. "Wake up, sleeper, and rise from death, and Christ will shine on you." Don't let anyone persuade you to rest short of the prize of your high calling in Christ Jesus. But cry to him day and night until you know in whom you have believed and can say, "My Lord and my God." Always pray and never become discouraged. You will one day be able to lift up your hands to heaven and declare to the One who lives for ever and ever, "Lord, you know everything; you know that I love you."

16. May we all come to experience what it is to be not almost only, but altogether Christians! Being justified [pardoned and relieved of the burden of sin] freely by God's grace, through the redemption that is in Jesus, knowing we have peace with God through Jesus Christ, rejoicing in hope of the glory of God, and having the love of God poured into our hearts by means of the Holy Spirit, who is God's gift to us!

17. Go out into the world, then, as a little child who believes in Jesus Christ. Though you are helpless and as vulnerable as an infant, the strongest of foes shall not be able to triumph over [your love]. Now thanks be to God who gives us the victory through our Lord Jesus Christ, to whom, with the Father and the Holy Ghost, be blessing and glory, and wisdom, and thanksgiving, and honor, and power, and might, for ever and ever. Amen.

3. ON GOD'S VINEYARD

Is there anything I failed to do for my vineyard? Then why did
it produce sour grapes and not the good grapes I expected?
(Isaiah 5:4)

1. The "vineyard of the Lord," taking the word in its widest sense, may include the whole world. In a narrower sense, it may mean the Christian world; that is, all that name the name of Christ. In a still narrower sense, it may be understood as the Protestant branch of the Christian church.

And in the narrowest sense of all, it may mean the body of people commonly called Methodists.

2. What more could God have done in this vineyard? What insight did God provide for them in matters of *doctrine?* What *aids* did God provide for their *spiritual growth?* What forms of *discipline* made them strong? What kind of *fruit* was produced from all of these efforts?

Doctrine

3. You could say that the Methodist movement first began when several Oxford University students and tutors joined together in order to find enrichment for their walk in Christ.[4] Each of these men determined that he would be a "man of one book" [*homo unius libri,*] namely, the Bible. The Word of God became their one rule, both of faith and of practice, i.e., the way in which they lived out that faith in their daily relationships.[5]

4. Disciplined study of scripture and the Christian classics led these earnest seekers after truth to a clearer understanding of the faith. They discovered, for instance, that growth in grace was inseparable from the experience of forgiveness—that faith and holiness belong together. They believed that the goal of life, which is nothing less than love of God and neighbor as Christ loved us, is directly related to the starting point of our journey in God's pardon of our sin. While faith is the means, love is the end of our life in Christ. And so, the Methodists maintain a balanced view of Christian vocation.

5. They are as tenacious of inward holiness as any mystic, and of outward holiness as any legalist. They believe that motives and actions

---

[4] John and Charles Wesley were among the members of this group and quickly emerged as its leaders. Some of their peers branded them the "Holy Club" because of the seriousness with which they took religion. Others described them as "Methodists" because of their disciplined life of personal piety and social service. All of these developments preceded Wesley's "evangelical conversion," his so-called heart-warming experience of Aldersgate in 1738. In spite of the monumental theological and personal changes of that year, Wesley's essential vision of a balanced Christian life, founded upon God's free grace for all, remained unchanged throughout the many years of his ministry.

[5] The remainder of this subdivision in the sermon is devoted to a lengthy discussion of justification by faith and sanctification in the Wesleyan understanding. Since we will examine these specific issues in detail in Chapter 2, I have omitted much of Wesley's argument here concerning these grand doctrines. In order to avoid premature exposure to undefined technical terms and concepts, some necessary liberties have been taken with the original text. The following two paragraphs represent a distillation of Wesley's viewpoint, expressed in a non-technical style and a more contemporary manner.

ought to be consistent. There must be a correlation between my personal experience of God's love in the depths of my heart and the expression of that love in the day-to-day relationships of my life. Who then is a Christian according to the light which God has given to this people? A Christian is anyone who, being "justified by faith, has peace with God through our Lord Jesus Christ."

Aids to Spiritual Growth

6. Two young clergymen (John and Charles Wesley), not very remarkable in any way, began to call sinners to repentance. The fruit of their preaching quickly appeared. Many sinners were changed both in heart and life. These clergymen had no plan at all. They only went wherever they had a prospect of saving souls. But when more and more asked, "What must I do to be saved?" they found it necessary to meet together in small groups.

7. Those who responded to their message of God's free grace for all were divided into cluster groups, or classes, according to where they lived. They appointed one person in each class to meet with all the rest on a weekly basis. In these small groups, the members became accountable to one another and assisted one another in their mutual endeavor to grow in grace. At that time, few communities had such a system of mutual accountability.

8. In order to increase the union between the preachers who cared for these expanding groups, they all met together for a special conference in London (in 1744). They spent a few days together in order to consider what might be done for the good of the movement. Soon they found that what Paul observes of the whole church may be, in a measure, applied to every part of it:

> The whole body is held together by every joint with which it is provided. So when each separate part works as it should, the whole body grows and builds itself up through love.
>
> (Ephesians 4:16, TEV)

9. God's whole design in raising up the people called Methodists was *to spread scriptural religion throughout the land*. People of other denominations are allowed to hold their own opinions and to follow their own mode of worship. For the primary aim of the Methodist people has always

been to renew the life of the world by proclaiming and living the message of faith working by love.

Discipline

10. The Methodist people are especially noted for their discipline. Nothing could be more simple, nothing more rational, than their system of caring for one another. It is entirely founded on common sense, particularly applying the general rules of scripture. Any person who wants to save his or her soul may be united with them. But evidence of this desire must be shown in three ways:

1. In their avoiding all known sin,
2. In their doing good according to their ability, and
3. In their attending all the ordinances of God (i.e., prayer, worship, the sacraments, the study of scripture).

11. Their public services of worship are at five in the morning, and six or seven in the evening. On Sunday it begins between nine and ten and concludes with the Lord's Supper. On Sunday evening the entire society meets. Once a quarter, the principal preacher in every circuit examines every member of the various societies. Whenever it is needful to exclude any disorderly members, it is done in the most quiet and inoffensive manner—only by not renewing their tickets at the quarterly visitation.[6]

The Consequences of Success

12. Every opinion, right or wrong, has been tolerated in almost every age. Every mode of worship has been tolerated, however superstitious or

[6] The "society," as we have seen, included members of all small groups under the direction of Wesley or his assistant in any given area. It was necessary for Wesley to group his rapidly expanding network of societies into geographical units for their spiritual supervision. Each of his assistants was appointed to and responsible for a number of societies in a particular region. He, and occasionally she, would visit each of the societies by means of a regular schedule of rounds. Societies linked together for this purpose became known as "circuits" because of the itinerant method of visitation. Every member of a class was issued a "ticket" to demonstrate his/her good-standing within the Methodist society structure. It was a sign of commitment to the vocation into which one felt called. So the quarterly renewal of these tickets was an important aspect of early Methodist discipline and a direct means of accountability.

absurd. But I do not know that true, vital, scriptural religion was ever tolerated before. The people called Methodists have abundant reason to praise God for the way in which earlier persecutions have died away. But the general acceptance of the revival has affected the movement in some dangerous ways.

13. Between forty and fifty years ago, I saw God's people alive in their first love. They magnified the Lord and rejoiced in God their Savior. I expected that all these would have lived like angels here below. I expected that they would have walked continually as if seeing and having constant communion with God. Living in eternity and walking in eternity I expected that they would continue to bear witness to the truth.

14. But instead of this, success brought forth wild grapes—fruit of a quite contrary nature. Particularly among those who have become wealthy as a result of their faithful stewardship, "success" has brought forth that grand poison of souls—the love of the world. O you that are rich in possessions, once more hear the Word of the Lord! You that are rich in this world, that have food to eat and clothing to wear, and much more than you need, are you safe from the curse of loving the world?

15. Are you aware of your danger? Do you realize how hard it is for those who have riches to enter the kingdom of God! Do you "put a knife to your throat" when you sit down to eat, lest your "table should be a snare to you"? Is not your belly your god? Are you not increasing in things, laying up treasures on earth, instead of restoring to God in the poor, not a little here and a little there, but all you can spare? Surely it is easier for a camel to go through the eye of a needle, than for a rich person to enter into God's realm of justice and peace.

16. But why will you still bring forth wild grapes? The whole Word of God has been proclaimed to you. The fundamental doctrines of God's pardoning love for you in Christ and of God's desire to restore you fully through the power of the Spirit have been preached repeatedly to you. Every aspect of both inward and outward holiness has been explained to you and applied directly to your lives.

17. Could it be that your falling away was caused by your failure to join together in fellowship with other disciples of Christ? Have you not read, "How can one be warm alone?" or "Woe be unto those who are alone when they fall?" Are your friends seekers after God? Do they encourage you to seek justice, and mercy, and peace? Do you have companions who watch over your soul as people who must give account? Do you have enough friends who freely and faithfully warn you if you take any false step or are in danger of doing so?

18. When you meet together in the name of the Lord, do you expect

him to be in the midst of you? Are you thankful to the giver of every good gift for the general spread of true religion? Surely, you can never praise God enough for all these blessings, so plentifully showered down upon you, until you praise the Lord with angels and archangels and all the company of heaven!

For Thought and Discussion

1. Reflect upon the three questions Wesley considered fundamental to Christian vocation: What to teach? How to teach? What to do? Formulate your own responses now, at the beginning of this study, to better grasp your present understanding of vocation. Write a paragraph on each question.

2. In the first quotation on page 4, Wesley describes religion as a "renewal of our minds," a "recovery of the Divine likeness," and a "conformity of heart and life" to Christ. What does he mean? Identify one example of renewal, one of recovery, and one of conformity in your own journey.

3. In his sermon on "The Almost Christian" (para. 10), Wesley defines faith. How does his definition correspond to or differ from your own understanding? Write or verbalize your own definition of faith.

4. Wesley claims that "every part of my life (not some only) must either be a sacrifice to God, or to myself; that is, in effect, to the devil" (p. 4). Read Romans 12:1-2. What in your life do you sacrifice the most, and to whom?

5. On pages 5-6, "The People Called Methodists," Wesley lists several important characteristics of fellowship. Again, in paragraph 3 of "On God's Vineyard," he emphasizes the importance of being "joined together." What opportunities do you have right now for Christian fellowship? In which do you participate, and why?

6. Paragraph 8 ("On God's Vineyard") considers the importance of discerning gifts for ministry. List three specific gifts which you possess. How is God challenging you to use them?

7. In "On God's Vineyard" (paras. 13-15), Wesley warns us about the dangers of "affluence." Read the story of the rich young man in Luke 18:18-27. Describe your immediate reaction to the story. List two specific actions you can take to be more faithful in your stewardship.

CHAPTER 2
WHAT TO TEACH

A. Introduction

The word *doctrine* has a sleep-inducing tone to it. For many people it conjures up the image of learned specialists haggling over minutiae. "I don't care about the Trinity," one critic complains. "Tell me how to find joy and meaning in life." In a pluralistic culture such as ours, others simply dismiss doctrine as the product of unenlightened minds. "It doesn't really matter what you believe," they say, "as long as you are sincere." Both criticisms point to the fact that doctrine, or theology, often seems quite detached from real life. It is something someone else does; it really doesn't touch my life at all.

In the early Wesleyan revival, however, doctrine—or *what to teach*— emerged as a primary concern at the foundational Conference of 1744. For the expanding movement to thrive and endure, Wesley realized that the seed of faith had to be planted in rich and carefully cultivated soil. He knew that the Christian community was called to be a clear expression of God's vision for a new age. For him, worship, doctrine, and life were intimately connected.

Christian vocation involves a challenge, therefore, to grow both in self-understanding and faithfulness. Action and reflection are essential to this kind of growth. The vitality of early Methodism was contagious, in part, because Wesley encouraged his followers to think through and share their experience of faith. Likewise, in our own time, each of us is invited to rediscover what it means

- To proclaim God's salvation,
- To live as a part of God's family, and
- To witness to God's grace in the world.

This is a theological task, and it necessarily engages the whole person in the community of faith.

The vocational issues addressed in this chapter focus upon

- Rediscovering the *hub of belief* in a pluralistic age,
- Understanding the *nature of salvation* by grace through faith, and
- Maintaining the balance of *personal faith and social witness*.

THE HUB OF BELIEF

The Body of Christ is like a richly textured and variously colored mosaic. Each particular facet within the pattern, by retaining its own unique features and dimensions, is essential to the beauty of the whole. Likewise, the Methodist family is a richly diverse community of faith. While we affirm our unity-in-diversity, it is never easy to maintain the integrity of this dynamic tension in our community. Unity without diversity is really uniformity; variety devoid of a unifying center is chaos. The question of *pluralism*, therefore, has become a hotly debated issue in our time.

Pluralism is a vocational issue because it begs the larger question: What is the heart of the gospel that I am called to proclaim and to live out in my own unique way within the context of my own tradition? What does it mean for any particular faith community to confess that Jesus Christ is Lord? What is the hub of belief *(kerygma)* around which community *(koinonia)* can be built and out of which service *(diakonia)* can extend?

Through the process of rediscovering who we are and what we believe, God can empower us to share our renewed vision in an ever-changing world.

THE NATURE OF SALVATION

At the heart of this quest is the obvious and perennial question, What is the nature of salvation? Your answer to this fundamental question will inform every aspect of your discipleship. It will reveal your basic attitude toward life, in all of its tragic and triumphant dimensions.

I will never forget an encounter I had with a faithful church member at the conclusion of a Lenten Bible study. She simply said: "I always had trouble understanding that business about salvation by grace. But once I experienced salvation as a gift, everything seemed clear and new." Today, we need to rediscover the transforming power of God's grace. We need a renewed understanding of faith in Christ as God's great gift to us. For this to happen, we must first be honest about our need and then enter the drama of God's action on our behalf.

PERSONAL FAITH AND SOCIAL WITNESS

The third vocational issue of the chapter has to do with the necessary connection between this personal experience of faith and our witness in a broken world. "Secret discipleship" is a contradiction in terms. Either the secrecy will make shipwreck of the discipleship, or true discipleship will find visible expression in dialogue with the burning issues of the day. Those who cling to personal faith and fail to apply it to the concerns of their brothers and sisters within the human family have lost their vision of mission. On the other hand, concern for society that is not rooted in vital faith is ultimately bankrupt and devoid of good news to share in a fragmented world. Personal and social dimensions of faith need to be held together.

Again, Wesley offers unique insights in each of these areas. He was not an "ivory tower" theologian. Rather, his ultimate concern was for the discovery of living, saving faith. Christian discipleship in the Wesleyan tradition, therefore, is a life of *faith seeking understanding.* It is a relationship that transforms people of bondage into the children of God.

Those doctrines which Wesley considered to be fundamental or "essential" are rooted in this dynamic, relational process, sometimes described as the *order of salvation.* The early Methodists joyously sang their theology because they had experienced the liberation of salvation by grace through faith. The central mission of the movement was to allow the light of Christ to shine through transformed lives to change the world for God.

The essence of Wesley's theology may be summarized in the phrase "faith working by love leading to holiness of heart and life." In the selections on *vital doctrine* that follow, you will encounter the basic components of this order of salvation. According to Wesley, the process of redemption revolved around three essential doctrines:

1. Original Sin
2. Justification by Faith
3. Sanctification

These core doctrines may be described as the fundamental *substance* of faith, or the faith *in which* one believes *(fides quae creditur)*. They were important to Wesley. But remember, it is the *act* of faith, or that living faith *by which* one believes *(fides qua creditur)*, that is primary in the vocation of every Christian. What is interesting is how active and reflective faith mutually interplay in order to help us grow. Within the worshiping community we receive and transmit this faith. As you read through the selections, think about how God's vision has formed you and how it has been informed by your reflection upon it.

Wesley's essential discovery concerning the Christian life is encapsulated in the classic text, Ephesians 2:8:

> For by grace you have been saved through faith; and this is not your own doing, it is the gift of God (RSV).

On June 11, 1738, shortly after his famous Aldersgate experience, he preached "Salvation by Faith" at St. Mary's Church in Oxford before the university community. This is the first of Wesley's "standard sermons." In 1765 he published a second sermonic-essay on this text, entitled "The Scripture Way of Salvation." This latter sermon is Wesley's definitive statement of God's free gift of faith working by love. It describes the dynamic balance of faith and holiness in the Christian life.

Wesley once described the collection of Jesus' teachings in the Sermon on the Mount as the sum of all true religion. The "standard sermons" include thirteen discourses on the Sermon as recorded in Matthew 5-7. In the Fourth Discourse (1748), Wesley challenges his reader to a life of Christian wholeness as the fruit of justifying faith. He characterizes Christianity as a "social religion" in which personal, saving faith is necessarily integrated with social, redemptive action. Life in Christ is both evangelical and ethical.

In his preaching and teaching Wesley sought to speak "plain words to plain people." As you explore the resources below, try to keep these simple definitions of key terms in mind:

Faith: the gift of trust in those things we cannot see, especially Christ's love for me

Repentance: a true self-understanding elicited by our vision of who we are in comparison to what we were created to be

Justification: the experience of having been accepted and pardoned by God through faith in Christ

Sanctification: the process of growing in grace and love

Perfection: the love of God and neighbor filling heart and life

B. Wesley Speaks

1. SELECTIONS ON THE DOCTRINES OF A LIVING FAITH

The Order of Salvation

Our main doctrines, which include all the rest, are three—that of repentance, of faith, and of holiness. The first of these we account as it were, the porch of religion; the next, the door; the third, religion itself.

(In a letter to Thomas Church, dated June 17, 1746)

Salvation begins with what is usually termed (and very properly) *preventing* grace; including the first wish to please God, the first dawn of light concerning his will, and the first slight transient conviction of having sinned against him. . . . Salvation is carried on by *convincing* grace, usually in Scripture termed repentance; which brings a larger measure of self-knowledge, and a farther deliverance from the heart of stone. Afterwards we experience the proper Christian salvation; whereby, "through grace," we "are saved by faith"; consisting of those two grand branches, justification and sanctification. By justification we are saved from the guilt of sin, and restored to the favor of God; by sanctification we are saved from the power and root of sin, and restored to the image of God.[7]

(In "On Working Out Our Own Salvation," 1785)

---

[7]The foundation of Wesley's order of salvation is the redemptive work of Christ and the revelation that our whole existence is enveloped by the wooing activity of God. The order of salvation itself is generally divided into the following states or events:

1. *Preventing, or Prevenient Grace* (a divine response to the fallenness of humanity) is universally operative and functions to stir the sinner to

2. *Repentance* (convincing grace, or true self-understanding). The sinner who has thereby come to himself/herself is reduced to despair which is the death of his or her working.

3. *Justification by faith alone* (justifying grace) is experienced in that moment as pardon

Original Sin

And in Adam all died, all humankind, all the children of men who were then in Adam's loins. The natural consequence of this is, that every one descended from him comes into the world spiritually dead, dead to God, wholly dead in sin; entirely void of the life of God; void of the image of God, of all that righteousness and holiness wherein Adam was created. . . . This then, is the foundation of the new birth—the entire corruption of our nature. Hence it is that being born in sin, we must be "born again."

(In "The New Birth," 1760)

Know thyself to be a sinner, and what manner of sinner thou art. Know that corruption of thy inmost nature, whereby thou art very far gone from original righteousness.

(In "The Way to the Kingdom," 1746)

Justification by Faith

If any doctrines within the whole compass of Christianity may be properly termed "fundamental," they are doubtless these two: the doctrine of *justification,* and that of the *new birth:* the former relating to that great work which God does *for us,* in forgiving our sins; the latter, to the great work which God does *in us,* in renewing our fallen nature.

(In "The New Birth," 1760)

Justification is another word for pardon. It is the forgiveness of all our sins; and, what is necessarily implied therein, our acceptance with God.

---

and a sure trust and confidence that "Christ died for me." It is the completion of the work which God had initiated by the activity of the Spirit in the life of the individual.

4. *Regeneration* or *New Birth* (a real change) is simultaneous with justification (a relative change). This new birth is the beginning of

5. *Sanctification* (sanctifying grace) or maturation into Scriptural Holiness, which is always characterized by the twin dimensions of

    a. holiness of heart (internal holiness) or Love of God, and

    b. holiness of life (external holiness) or Love of Neighbor.

The goal of this whole process is

6. *Perfect Love* (entire sanctification or Christian Perfection) as the Spirit's greatest gift.

None of these stages is static; rather they represent a dynamic, relational process of faith working by love leading to holiness of heart and life.

The price whereby this hath been procured for us . . . is the blood and righteousness of Christ.

(In "Justification by Faith," 1746)

Neither our faith nor our works justify us, that is, deserve the remission of our sins. But God himself justifies us, of his own mercy, through the merits of his Son only. . . . Our corruption through original sin is so great, that all our faith, charity, words, and works, cannot merit or deserve any part of our justification for us.

(In "The Principles of a Methodist," 1740. Wesley is arguing here for salvation as a gift and not as an achievement.)

"Come to me" . . . I alone (for none else can) *will* freely *give you* (what you cannot purchase) *rest* from the guilt of sin by justification.

(In "Notes on the New Testament" [Matt. 11:28], 1755)

> Long my imprisoned spirit lay,
>   Fast bound in sin and nature's night;
> Thine eye diffused a quickening ray;
>   I woke, the dungeon flamed with light;
> My chains fell off, my heart was free,
>   I rose, went forth, and followed thee.
> *(In Charles Wesley's hymn, "And Can It Be")*

Sanctification

[Faith] is the grand means of restoring that holy love wherein man was originally created. It follows, that although faith is of no value in itself (as neither is any other means whatsoever), yet as it leads to that end, the establishing anew the law of love in our hearts.

(In "The Law Established Through Faith, II," 1750. In Wesley's theology there is a direct relationship between creation and redemption. Through Christ, God restores to humanity all that was lost in the fall.)

[Sanctification] begins the moment we are justified, in the holy, humble, gentle, patient love of God and man. It gradually increases from that moment, as "a grain of mustard-seed, which, at first, is the

least of all seeds," but afterwards puts forth large branches, and becomes a great tree; till, in another instant, the heart is cleansed from
all sin, and filled with pure love to God and man. But even that love
increases more and more, till we "grow up in all things into Him that is
our Head"; till we attain "the measure of the stature of the fulness of
Christ."

(In "On Working Out Our Own Salvation," 1785)

This much is certain: they that love God with all their heart and all
men as themselves are scripturally perfect. And surely such there are;
otherwise the promise of God would be a mere mockery of human weak-
ness. Hold fast this. But then remember, on the other hand, you have this
treasure in an earthen vessel; you dwell in a poor, shattered house of clay,
which presses down the immortal spirit. Hence all your thoughts, words,
and actions are so imperfect, so far from coming up to the standard . . .
that you may well say till you go to Him you love: Every moment, Lord, I
need the merit of your death.

(In a letter to Miss March, dated April 7, 1763)

What is religion then? It is easy to answer, if we consult [the
Bible]. . . . It lies in one single point: it is neither more nor less than
love. It is the love which "is the fulfilling of the law, the end of the
commandments." Religion is the love of God and our neighbor; that is,
every man under heaven.

(In "The Important Question," September 11, 1775)

2. THE SCRIPTURE WAY OF SALVATION

For it is by God's grace that you have been saved through faith.
It is not the result of your own efforts, but God's gift.
(Ephesians 2:8, TEV)

1. The true religion of Jesus Christ is plain and simple. The end of
religion is, in one word, *salvation;* the means to attain it, *faith.* These two
words contain the substance of the gospel. In this sermon we will explore
what salvation is, what that faith is by which we are saved, and how we are
saved by it.

What Is Salvation?

2. Salvation is not merely going to heaven or looking forward to eternal happiness. It is a present reality, a blessing which you may possess now through the free mercy of God. Salvation here refers to the entire work of God, from the first dawning of grace in the soul to its consummation in glory. But the two main parts of salvation, according to the apostle, are *justification* and *sanctification*.

3. *Justification* is another word for pardon. It is the forgiveness of all our sins and, what is necessarily implied, our acceptance with God. The price by which this has been purchased for us is nothing less than the blood and righteousness of Christ. The immediate effect of justification is the peace of God. It is a peace which passes all understanding and a "rejoicing in hope of the glory of God."

4. At the same time that we are justified, in that very moment, *sanctification* begins. In that instant we are "born again, born from above, born of the Spirit." There is a real as well as a relative change. We are inwardly renewed by the power of God. So from the time of our being "born again," the gradual work of sanctification takes place. We are more and more dead to sin, and more and more alive to God.

5. The apostle describes this process as "going on to perfection." But what is *perfection?* The word has various senses. Here it means "perfect love." It is love excluding sin, love filling the heart, taking up the whole capacity of the soul. It is love "rejoicing ever more, praying without ceasing, in everything giving thanks."

What Is Saving Faith?

6. Faith, in general, is defined by the apostle as "a certainty in those things we cannot see" (Heb. 11:1). To have faith is to trust in God, to be "sure of the things we hope for." It is a kind of spiritual "light" and supernatural "sight" or perception. It is a gift through which we receive Christ in all of his offices as our Prophet, Priest, and Lord.

7. In a more particular sense, faith is a certainty, not only that "God was in Christ, reconciling the world to himself" (rsv), but also that "Christ loved me and gave himself for me." Faith necessarily implies an "assurance" of these things. Because of the nature of human experience, the assurance goes before the certainty. For no one can have a childlike trust in God until he or she experiences adoption as a child of God. It is through this gift of faith that we are saved.

How Are We Saved by Faith?

8. First, how are we *justified by faith?* Faith is the only thing necessary for justification. No one is justified unless he or she believes; without faith no one is justified. But whenever any one believes, that person is justified. People may repent, but they are not justified until they believe. The moment they do believe, with or without previous repentance, they are justified. One can say, therefore, that repentance and its fruits are only remotely necessary, whereas faith is immediately and directly necessary to justification.

9. Second, I have continually testified in private and in public that we are *sanctified* as well as justified *by faith.* Exactly as we are justified by faith, so are we sanctified by faith. Without faith, no person is sanctified; any person is sanctified as soon as he/she believes. It is necessary, however, for all who are justified to be active in good works. For without them no one can "grow in grace," in the image of God, or in the mind which was in Christ. In fact, without good works, God's children cannot retain the grace they have received.

10. Both repentance, rightly understood, and the practice of good works are, in some sense, necessary to sanctification. But repentance following the experience of justification is widely different from that which precedes it. It is properly a conviction of the "sin" which still "remains" in our heart but which no longer "reigns." It is a conviction of our continuing proneness to evil even after we have been found by God. A conviction of our continuing helplessness is also implied in this repentance. It is a realization that God's free grace comes before any of our inclinations to do what is good, and then accompanies us every moment.

11. But what good works are necessary to sanctification? First, all works of piety such as public, family, and private prayer, receiving the Lord's Supper, searching the scriptures by hearing, reading, meditating, and using fasting as our bodily health allows. Second, all works of mercy, whether they relate to people's physical or spiritual needs: feeding the hungry, clothing the naked, entertaining the stranger, visiting those that are in prison or are sick, endeavoring to instruct the ignorant; attempting to awaken sinners, to revive the lukewarm, to confirm those who waver, to comfort those who are discouraged, to be accountable for all in your care. This is the way wherein God has appointed his children to wait for complete salvation.

12. Because of this, there is extreme danger in the seemingly innocent opinion that there is no sin in a believer. Some believe that all sin is destroyed, root and branch, the moment a person is justified [or saved].

By neglecting the form of repentance that is necessary following justification, the way to sanctification is actually blocked. [There is no room for growth in grace subsequent to conversion in such a view.]

13. As with justification, both this repentance and its fruits are necessary for full salvation. [They are important means toward the end of loving God and neighbor as Christ has loved us.] But they are not necessary either in the same sense as faith, or in the same degree. Only faith is immediately and directly necessary to sanctification.

14. What is that faith, then, by which we are sanctified, saved from sin, and perfected in love? It is a certainty that God has promised it in the Holy Scriptures, that what God has promised the Spirit is able to realize in the lives of God's children. It is a certainty that God is willing and able to do it now, and that God does it. The believer experiences the deep meaning of those solemn words:

> If we live in the light—just as he is in the light—then we have fellowship with one another, and the blood of Jesus, his Son, purifies us from every sin (1 John 1:7, TEV).

15. If you see the fullness of salvation by faith, you may expect it as you are, and if as you are, then expect it now. There is an inseparable connection between these three points:

> Expect it *by faith;*
> Expect it *as you are;*
> And expect it *now.*

To deny one of them is to deny them all. To allow one is to allow them all.

16. Do you believe we are sanctified by faith? Be true then to your principle and look for this blessing just as you are, neither better nor worse. As a poor sinner you still have nothing to pay, nothing to plead but "Christ died." And if you look for it as you are, then expect it now. Christ is ready and he is all you want. He is waiting for you! He is at the door! Let your inmost soul cry out:

> Come in, come in, thou heavenly Guest!
> Nor hence again remove;
> But sup with me and let the feast
> Be everlasting love.

3. UPON OUR LORD'S SERMON ON THE MOUNT, IV

*You are like salt for all humankind. But if salt loses its saltiness,
there is no way to make it salty again. It has become worthless, so it
is thrown out and people trample on it. You are like light for the
whole world. A city built on a hill cannot be hid. No one lights a
lamp and puts it under a bowl; instead he puts it on the lampstand,
where it gives light for everyone in the house. In the same way your
light must shine before people, so that they will see the good things
you do and praise your Father in heaven.*

(Matthew 5:13-16, TEV)

1. In order to explain these important words I shall endeavor to show,
first, that Christianity is essentially a social religion, and that to turn it
into a solitary one is to destroy it; and second, that to conceal this
religion is impossible, as well as utterly contrary to the design of its
author. I shall, third, answer some objections and conclude with a
practical application.

Social Religion

2. By Christianity I mean that life of witness, service, and praise
revealed to us by Jesus Christ. When I say this is essentially a social
religion, I mean not only that it cannot exist very well, but that it cannot
exist at all apart from fellowship and witness. It requires [a loving and
sharing community in mission]. To turn Christianity into a religion that
can be lived out in isolation is to destroy it.

3. This, however, is not a condemnation of solitude. Time for personal
and private reflection is not only allowable, but expedient. It is absolutely
necessary, as daily experience shows, for everyone who desires to be a real
Christian. We all need to retreat daily from the world, at least morning
and evening, in order to pray and to be nourished by intimate communion with God.

4. But solitude must not swallow up all our time; this would be to
destroy, not advance, true religion. There is no virtue, for instance, which
is more essential to Christianity than meekness. But to turn this into a
solitary virtue is to destroy it. Another important aspect of true Christianity is peacemaking. Will anyone affirm that a solitary Christian can be
an ambassador of reconciliation and mercy? How can a person isolated

from other people grasp every opportunity of doing all good to all people? It is obvious that the religion of Jesus Christ cannot possibly exist without these social dimensions.

5. It is your very nature to season whatever is around you. It is the nature of the divine savor which is in you to spread to whatever you touch. This is the great reason why the providence of God brings us all into contact with so many other people, that whatever grace we have received may be communicated to them through us. Every holy temper, and word, and work of yours may have an influence on others that you will never know.

6. If you were once excited about your life with God, and consequently anxious to help others find happiness in life, but have lost your saltiness and no longer season others—if you are grown flat, insipid, dead, both careless of your own soul and useless to the souls of others—how is your saltiness to be restored? How shall you be recovered? What help is there? What hope? Can tasteless salt be restored to its savor?

Bearing Witness to the Light

7. Some may argue that salt conveys its savor without any noise. And if so, even though we do not go out of the world, may we not lie hidden in it? May we not keep our religion to ourselves and not offend those whom we cannot help? So long as true religion—the religion of Jesus Christ—abides in our hearts, it is impossible to conceal it! To hide the light that God gives to us would be absolutely contrary to the design of its great author.

8. Your holiness makes you as conspicuous as the sun in the midst of heaven. As you cannot go out of the world, so neither can you stay in it without appearing to all humankind. You may not flee from others, and while you are among them it is impossible to hide your lowliness and meekness and those other virtues by which you aspire to be perfect. Love cannot be hid any more than light; and least of all when it shines forth in action. Your patient and unwearied efforts to show love and mercy, to overcome evil with good, will make you still more visible and conspicuous than you were before.

9. If your religion can be concealed, it is not Christianity. Never, therefore, let it enter into the hearts of those whom God has renewed in the spirit of their minds to hide that light. It is impossible for you to keep your religion to yourself. You cannot conceal true Christianity because of its very design.

10. It is hard to imagine any arguments against this clear view. After all that scripture and reason have said, however, some of the arguments for solitary religion do seem to be exceedingly plausible. We need all the wisdom of God, therefore, to see through the snare. For many and strong are the objections that have been raised against a social, open, and active faith.

OBJECTIONS TO SOCIAL RELIGION

11. First, it has been objected that religion does not lie in outward things but in the heart, the inmost soul, and that outward religion is worthless. Certainly the root of religion does lie in the heart, but if the root is truly alive within, it will produce good fruit that is visible to everyone. While it is also true that bare, outward religion in itself is worthless, God delights in that genuine love and service which is the product of a pure and holy heart. God is pleased with the sacrifice of our prayers of praise and thanksgiving, with the sacrifice of our goods, when humbly devoted to God and used for the glory of Christ.

12. Second, some object that all anybody needs is love. It is granted that the love of God and neighbor which springs from living faith is all God requires for the fulfilling of the law. Without this, whatever we do or suffer is of no value. But it does not follow that love is an end in itself such that it supersedes either faith or good works. No! God has joined them together from the beginning of the world. And let no one put them asunder.

13. Since "God is a Spirit," others object, we must worship God "in spirit and in truth." Is this not enough, they argue? Yes, it is, but what does it mean to worship God in spirit and in truth? It is to believe in God as a wise, just, holy being; and yet merciful, gracious, and long-suffering. It is to love God, to delight in God, to desire God, with all our heart and mind and soul and strength; to imitate Christ whom we love by purifying ourselves, even as he is pure; and to obey him whom we love, and in whom we believe, both in thought and word and deed. Consequently, you cannot worship God correctly without keeping God's commandments. To glorify God with our bodies as well as our spirits, to practice good deeds with hearts lifted up to our Lord, to make our daily work a sacrifice to God is to offer our spiritual worship as a return of gratitude.

14. The grand objection, however, is the appeal to experience. Our light did shine, some would say; we used outward things many years and it

made no difference. I know that many have abused the ordinances of God, mistaking the means for the end of religion. Many suppose that [attending church and receiving the sacraments, or simply trying to be good] either was the religion of Jesus Christ or would be accepted in its place. But let the abuse be taken away and the use remain! Now use all those outward forms in which God has promised to meet you. But use them with a constant eye to the renewal of your soul in righteousness and true holiness.

A Practical Application

15. "Let your light shine"—your lowliness of heart, your gentleness and meekness of wisdom; your serious, weighty concern for the things of eternity, and sorrow for the sins and miseries of all people; your earnest desire for universal holiness and full happiness in God; your tender goodwill to all your brothers and sisters, and fervent love to God. Let it shine still more eminently in your actions, in your doing all possible good to all people and in your suffering for righteousness' sake.

16. Only be careful not to seek your own praise. Avoid any desire to honor yourself. But let it be your sole aim that all who see your good works may "glorify your Father in heaven." Make this your one ultimate end in all things. Be plain, open, and undisguised in living out this central purpose. Be honest and sincere in your dealings with all people that they may see the grace of God which is in you. And although some will harden their hearts, others will perceive that you have been with Jesus.

17. Let the light which is in your heart shine in all good works, both works of piety and works of mercy. In order to enlarge your ability of doing good, renounce all luxuries. Cut off all unnecessary expense, in food, in furniture, and in clothing. Be a good steward of every gift of God. In a word, be full of faith and love; do good; suffer evil. In your efforts to live by faith be steadfast and unmoveable.

For Thought and Discussion

1. Compile a list (at most five) of your own "vital doctrines." Briefly describe why each doctrine is important to you?

2. In his hymn (p. 23), Charles Wesley describes justification as a liberating experience. In what ways has Christ freed you? Relate two experiences from your own faith pilgrimage.

3. The quotations on pages 23-24 describe a process of "going on to perfection." Some people view holiness in terms of right actions. What you *do* determines whether you are holy or not. Others conceive of holiness from the standpoint of motives. Holiness is where your *heart* is. Choose one of these positions and try to defend it.

4. According to Wesley, what is necessary for our growth in grace (See "Scripture Way of Salvation," paras. 11-12)? Name two items you would add to the list.

5. What kind of a God is revealed to you in the concluding paragraphs of the "Scripture Way of Salvation" (paras. 15-16)? What kinds of adjectives would you use to describe this God?

6. What is social religion in paragraphs 2-4 of Wesley's "Sermon on the Mount, IV,"? When do you find solitude? Describe a situation in which solitude has enhanced personal relationships in your own experience.

7. Wesley claims that "if your religion can be concealed, it is not Christianity." Reread "Sermon on the Mount, IV," paragraphs 7-9. Describe one person in whom you have encountered the light of Christ. What makes him/her unique?

8. Review the practical suggestions offered in paragraph 17 of "Sermon on the Mount, IV." Make your own list of four specific resolutions, beginning each statement with the words: "Relying on God's grace, this week I hope to reflect the light of Christ by. . . ."

CHAPTER 3
HOW TO TEACH

A. Introduction

The church is always in need of reform, and renewal often seems radical. Indeed, "radical" literally means to go to the center or the source of something, to rediscover the root *(radix)*. So renewal always sparks a new passion among Christ's disciples to get back to basics, to unearth the roots of our faith. It is not surprising, then, that those aspects of the faith being rediscovered today are the classic elements of renewal:

- Emphasis upon the experiential side of faith and personal relationship with God through Christ
- Rediscovery of the Bible as the "living Word" and as the "book of the people"
- Elevation of the ministry of the laity as an essential expression of the priesthood of all believers
- Stress upon mutual accountability and the strength drawn from intimate community (small groups)
- Celebration of classical spiritual disciplines as important means both of conversion and growth
- Renewed interest in the sacramental life of the church and liturgy as the "work of the people"

In all of this, the dynamic balance of life and Spirit, Spirit and Word, Word and sacrament, sacrament and life has become a vital means to the rediscovery of living faith.

These elements of renewal constitute spiritual formation. This new emphasis within the church is a pressing vocational issue. We know now that we cannot meet the challenges of our age without strong inner resources. Activities and programs cannot substitute for well-formed spiritual beings.

33

Moreover, the way in which we communicate our faith must unite our concern for both individuals and society with a holistic understanding of people as thinking, feeling, and acting beings. To transmit the faith from one generation to the next means to help people understand, experience, and act upon the good news of Jesus Christ. This is central to the mission of the church. Spiritual formation, therefore, prepares the committed disciple to "live God's Word" in the world; and this is what Christian vocation is all about.

MEANS OF GRACE

As in all previous periods of renewal, the church today is rediscovering the power of the eucharist. Since the second century and possibly in the New Testament itself, this term has referred to the sacrament of Holy Communion. Literally meaning "thanksgiving," the eucharist has always been a vital, if not central, force in the formation of Christ's disciples. In the sacrament, we realize the unity of the individual and the community, reflection and action, cross and resurrection, remembrance and thanksgiving.

The power of the sacrament partially rests in the capacity of sign-acts to communicate the fullness of God's love and grace to the whole person. Words and signs, senses and action all combine through the power of the Holy Spirit to make the eucharist a genuine place of divine encounter. It is the "visible Word" which confronts and comforts us in those areas of life the "spoken Word" cannot reach.

I know of a young woman, for instance, who struggled for two years over the death of her father. That loss in her life left a void that could not be filled. On All Saints' Day she participated in a memorable Communion service that transformed her despair into triumphant joy. After the service, hugging the pastor, she said:

I have never felt as close to my father as I did today when I thanked God for his life. It was almost as if I could reach out and touch him. Now I know that he is with me; I never have to feel alone again.

At the eucharist she experienced reconciliation.

Likewise, the words of a youth, written in a letter to her former pastor, reveal the transforming power of this newly rediscovered means of grace:

> When I received the bread and wine, I felt that I had found Christ, really found him, for the first time in my life. I can honestly say that receiving the Holy Communion has become the most important part of the worship service for me.

Like this young disciple, many people today are pointing to the eucharist as that place where God reminds us of who and whose we are, feeds us for our journey, and unites us in service to the world.

Methodism was, above all else, a movement of spiritual renewal within the life of the church. It was Wesley's concern with reform that prompted his question about *how to teach*. How does the church offer Christ, offer God's grace, to a world in need of re-creation? Where do we encounter God? How can we find, or rather, how can we be found by God? How do we communicate the wonders of God's love which we have experienced in life?

Wesley's simple answer to these questions was that we encounter God in those places Christ promised to be present. We call these places the "means of grace." It is through these means that God transforms our lives, forms our spirits, and informs our action. We encounter the "living Word" as the Spirit breathes life into the words of scripture; when two or three are gathered in his name, Christ is in their midst; God meets us at the table and at our place of prayer to commune with us and empower us to serve.

In general, for Wesley there are five chief means of grace. By means of (1) prayer, (2) Word (read, preached, and meditated upon), (3) fasting, (4) Christian conference (what we might call "fellowship"), and (5) the Lord's Supper, God gives and preserves a life of faith and holiness. As you read through the selections on these places of divine/human encounter, consider how your life has been changed and enriched by them. Have these been places where you have discovered the living Lord?

The Wesleyan revival of the eighteenth century was both evangelical and sacramental. The experience of the early Methodists brought about a rediscovery of the dynamic interrelation of Word and sacrament. Sacramental grace and evangelical experience were viewed as necessary counterparts of a balanced Christian life. The enthusiasm for Holy Communion among the early Methodists was the result of zeal kindled in the hearts of the people by the flaming message of God's love. And so, the two-edged sword of Word and sacrament became a potent agent in the spread of the revival. It is not too much to say that the unity of rich personal faith and abundant relational grace was the vital center of the Wesleyan message.

In 1787, when many Methodists were advocating "infrequent communion," Wesley republished a fifty-five-year-old sermon which enjoined "Constant Communion" upon his faithful disciples. He viewed the Lord's Supper as the chief means of grace, the greatest example and grandest channel of God's love in action. His conception of the sacrament was profoundly relational. Not only was it an indispensable means of grace to individuals; it was also a potent social symbol. It was the place at which belief and life met, the truest expression of doxology. Wesley's dynamic balance of sacramental grace and evangelical experience is yet another instance of his unique ability to bring vitality to responsible discipleship.

Christian vocation, if it is to be Wesleyan, must be rooted in the means of grace; spiritual formation that is true to the Wesleyan tradition will be eucharistic. Through these means God communicates the love revealed to us in Christ. Through them we learn of him and grow into his likeness.

B. Wesley Speaks

1. SELECTIONS ON THE PLACES OF DIVINE/HUMAN ENCOUNTER

The End and Means of Grace

All the externals of religion are in order to the renewal of our soul in righteousness and true holiness. But it is not true that the external way is one and the internal way another. There is but one scriptural way wherein we receive inward grace—through the outward means which God hath appointed.

(In a letter to William Law, dated January 6, 1756)

By "means of grace," I understand outward signs, words, or actions, ordained of God, and appointed for this end, to be the ordinary channels whereby He might convey to men, preventing, justifying, or sanctifying grace.

(In "The Means of Grace," 1746. The means of grace are intimately related to the order of salvation discussed in the previous chapter.)

One general inlet to enthusiasm is the expecting the end without the means—the expecting knowledge, for instance, without searching the

Scripture and consulting the children of God; the expecting spiritual strength without constant prayer; the expecting growth in grace without steady watchfulness and deep self-examination; the expecting any blessing without hearing the Word of God at every opportunity.

(In "Cautions and Directions," 1762)

Prayer

To the public, constantly add the private means of grace, particularly prayer and reading. Most of you have been greatly wanting in this; and without this you can never grow in grace. You may as well expect a child to grow without food as a soul without private prayer.

(In a letter "To the Societies at Bristol," 1764)

Prayer is the lifting up of the heart to God: all words of prayer, without this are mere hypocrisy. Whenever therefore thou attemptest to pray, see that it be thy one design to commune with God, to lift up thy heart to Him, to pour out thy soul before Him, not as hypocrites, who love, or are wont "to pray standing in the synagogues . . .that they may be seen of men."

(In "Upon Our Lord's Sermon on the Mount, VI," 1748)

The Role of the Word

I showed concerning the Holy Scriptures: That to search (that is, read and hear them) is a command of God. . . . That this is commanded or ordained as a means of grace, a means of conveying the grace of God to all, whether unbelievers . . .or believers, who by experience know that "all Scripture is profitable," or a means to this end, "that the man of God may be perfect, thoroughly furnished to all good works."

(In the Journal, Thurs., June 26, 1740)

Fasting

[Fasting] has so frequently been found a means in the hand of God, of confirming and increasing not one virtue, not chastity only . . . but also seriousness of spirit, earnestness, sensibility and tenderness of conscience, deadness to the world, and consequently the love of God, and every holy and heavenly affection.

(In "Upon Our Lord's Sermon on the Mount, VII," 1748)

Christian Conference

Holy Solitaries is a phrase no more consistent with the gospel than Holy Adulterers. The Gospel of Christ knows of no Religion, but Social; no Holiness but Social Holiness.

(In the Preface to "Hymns and Sacred Poems," 1739)

Eucharist: The Visible Word

I showed at large: (1) That the Lord's Supper was ordained by God to be a means of conveying to me either preventing, or justifying, or sanctifying grace, according to their several necessities. (2) That the persons for whom it was ordained are all those who know and feel that they want the grace of God.

(In the Journal, dated Saturday, June 28, 1740. Again Wesley shows how this chief means of grace is directly related to the order of salvation. God meets us in the means of grace at our point of need.)

The grace of God given herein confirms to us the pardon of our sins, and enables us to leave them. As our bodies are strengthened by bread and wine, so are our souls by these tokens of the body and blood of Christ. This is the food of our souls: This gives strength to perform our duty, and leads us on to perfection.

(In "The Duty of Constant Communion," 1787)

She had long earnestly desired to receive the Holy communion, having an unaccountably strong persuasion that God would manifest Himself to her therein, and give rest to her soul. . . . And "He was made known unto her in the breaking of bread." In that moment she felt her load removed, she knew she was accepted in the Beloved.

(In the Journal, dated Thursday, September 20, 1739. The woman to whom Wesley refers was his mother, Susanna Wesley. Her experience at the Sacrament was

reduplicated in the lives of countless Methodists and greatly influenced Wesley's understanding of the eucharist.)

Fasting He doth, and hearing bless,
    And prayer can much avail,
Good vessels all to draw the grace
    Out of salvation's well.

But none, like this mysterious rite
    Which dying mercy gave,
Can draw forth all His promised might
    And all His will to save.

This is the richest legacy
    Thou hast on man bestow'd:
Here chiefly, Lord, we feed on Thee,
    And drink Thy precious blood.

The prayer, the fast, the word conveys,
    When mix'd with faith, Thy life to me;
In all the channels of Thy grace
    I still have fellowship with Thee:
But chiefly here my soul is fed
    With fulness of immortal bread.
           (In "Hymns on the Lord's Supper," 1745)

Before you use any means, let it be deeply impressed on your soul—there is no power in this. It is, in itself, a poor, dead, empty thing: separate from God, it is a dry leaf, a shadow. . . . But, because God bids, therefore I do; because He directs me to wait in this way, therefore here I wait for His free mercy, whereof cometh my salvation . . .use all means as means; as ordained, not for their own sake, but in order to the renewal of your soul in righteousness and true holiness.
           (In "The Means of Grace," 1746)

2. THE MEANS OF GRACE

You, like your ancestors before you, have turned away
from my laws and have not kept them.
(Malachi 3:7, TEV)

1. Are there any "means" ordained by God as the usual channels of saving grace? This question could never have been proposed in the early church. The whole body of Christians believed that Christ had ordained certain outward means for conveying his grace to the children of God. Their constant practice set this beyond all dispute. "All that believed continued steadfastly in the teaching of the apostles, and in the breaking of bread, and in prayers."

2. In the following sermon, I propose to examine whether there are any means of grace. By means of grace I mean *outward signs, words, or actions ordained by God* and appointed to be *the ordinary channels by which God conveys preventing, justifying, and sanctifying grace* to persons in search of life.

Primary Channels of Grace

The chief of these channels of grace are prayer, whether in private or within the context of worship; searching the scriptures (which implies reading, hearing, and meditating upon them); and receiving the Lord's Supper, eating bread and drinking wine in remembrance of him. These we believe to be ordained of God as the ordinary means by which God relates to us and offers the grace of Christ through the power of the Holy Spirit.

4. The whole value of these means depends on their actual subservience to the end of religion. All these means, if separated from their end, are less than nothing and vanity. If they do not lead to the knowledge and love of God, they are not acceptable in God's sight; rather, they are an abomination—a stink in God's nostrils. Whoever imagines there is any intrinsic power in the means themselves is in great error. For we know that there is no inherent power in the words that are spoken in prayer, in the letter of scripture read, or the bread and wine received in the Lord's Supper.

5. It is God alone who is the giver of every good gift. It is only owing to God that there is any blessing conveyed to our souls through any of these

means. Indeed, the great foundation of the whole Christian building is that of salvation by grace through faith. You are saved from your sins and restored to the favor and image of God, not by any works, merits, or deservings of your own, but by the free grace, the mere mercy of God through the merits of God's well-beloved Son.

6. But the main question remains. If salvation is the gift and the work of God, how may I attain it? Our Lord has shown us the way in the Word! According to holy scripture, all who desire the grace of God are to wait for it in the means which God has ordained; in using, not in laying them aside.

Prayer

7. First, all who desire the grace of God are to wait for it in the way of prayer. This is the express direction of our Lord himself. In his Sermon on the Mount he enjoins: "Ask, and you will receive; seek, and you will find; knock, and the door will be opened to you" (TEV). How could our blessed Lord more plainly declare that we may enrich our relationship with God by this means.

Searching the Scriptures

8. Second, you are to wait for God's grace in searching the scriptures. Our Lord's direction with regard to the use of this means is equally plain and clear. "Search the Scriptures," he says to the unbelieving Jews, "for they testify of me." He directed them to study the Word in order that they might believe in him.

9. God richly blesses those who read and meditate upon the Word. Through this means God not only gives, but also confirms and increases true wisdom. Paul admonished Timothy: "Ever since you were a child, you have known the Holy Scriptures, which are able to give you the wisdom that leads to salvation through faith in Christ Jesus" (TEV). How far then was Paul from making light of the Old Testament. He found power and light in the wholeness of scripture. If you read, study, and value the totality of God's Word, you will not wander and perish. Let all, therefore, who desire that day of salvation to dawn upon their hearts, wait for it in searching the scriptures.

The Lord's Supper

10. Third, all who desire an increase of the grace of God are to wait for it in partaking of the Lord's Supper. In this too, Jesus' direction is clear:

> For I received from the Lord the teaching that I passed on to you: that the Lord Jesus, on the night he was betrayed, took a piece of bread, gave thanks to God, broke it, and said, "This is my body, which is for you. Do this in memory of me" (TEV).

The command first given by our Lord is expressly repeated by the apostle: "Let everyone eat; let everyone drink." These words not only imply a bare permission, but a clear and explicit command.

11. Is not the eating of that bread, and the drinking of that cup, the outward and visible means by which God conveys that inward and spiritual grace to our lives? God offers to us that righteousness and peace and joy in the Holy Spirit that was purchased by the body of Christ once broken and the blood of Christ once shed for us! Let all, therefore, who truly desire the grace of God, eat of that bread and drink of that cup!

Objections Answered

12. Many people have raised objections against the use of these means of grace. The first and chief of these is: "You cannot use these means without trusting in them." But what do you mean by trusting in them? Believing that if I wait in this way I shall attain what otherwise I should not? By the grace of God I will thus trust in them till the day of my death. I will believe that whatever God has promised God is faithful also to perform. And seeing God has promised to bless me in this way, I trust it shall be according to the Word.

13. Second, some say that this is seeking salvation by works. But what is seeking salvation by works? In the writings of Paul it means either seeking to be saved by observing the ritual works of the Old Testament Law or expecting salvation for the sake of our own works, by the merit of our own righteousness. But how is either of these implied in my waiting in the way God has ordained, by expecting to meet God where God has promised to be?

14. Third, some vehemently object that Christ is the only means of

grace. When you say that Christ is the means of grace, you mean that he is the sole price and purchaser of it. But who denies this! Seeing that grace is the gift of God, we are undoubtedly to wait on God for salvation. But if God has appointed a way for us to wait, can you devise a better plan? That great truth must stand unshaken: all who desire the grace of God are to wait for it in the means which God has ordained.

Directions on Using the Means:
The Proper Order

15. It is important to know how to use the means properly with regard, first, to order. There is a kind of natural order by which God usually employs these means in bringing a sinner to salvation. God often encounters people or confronts them when they least expect it. Someone may be awakened by a sermon or conversation, by a tragedy, or by an immediate stroke of the convincing Spirit. The seeker purposely goes to *hear* how he or she may be saved. Hearing and reading the scripture leads to more intentional meditation.

16. Such persons begin to talk about the things of God and to pray. They want to pray with those who know God. In worship they notice others who go to the Table of the Lord. They consider that Christ said, "Do this." After struggling with their scruples: I am too great a sinner; I am not fit; I am not worthy; they break through. They continue in God's way—in hearing, reading, meditating, praying, and partaking of the Lord's Supper—until God speaks to their heart through the power of the Spirit: "Your faith has saved you; go in peace."

17. Our understanding of this natural progression can help us in leading persons step by step through the means. [An understanding of the stages of faith should inform our discussion in these spiritual matters and guide us in our recommendations.] Yet as we find no command in scripture for any particular order to be observed, so neither do the providence and the Spirit of God adhere to any, without variation. The means into which different people are led and in which they find the blessing of God, are varied, transposed, and combined together a thousand different ways.

18. The sure and general rule for all who groan for salvation is this: Whenever opportunity serves, use all the means which God has ordained. For who knows in which God will meet you with the grace that brings salvation?

Directions on Using the Means:
The Proper Manner

19. With regard to the proper manner of using the means, it is important to remember that God is always above all means. Do not limit the Almighty. God can convey the grace of Christ either in or outside any of the means that have been appointed. Look then every moment for God's appearing! God is always ready; always willing; always able to save!

20. Second, before you use any means, consider carefully that there is no power in this alone. The means are in themselves poor, dead, empty things. Separate from God every means is a dry leaf, a shadow. Neither is there any merit in your using them; nothing intrinsically pleasing to God. But because God bids, therefore I do. Because God directs me to wait in this way, therefore I wait here for God's free mercy and love.

21. Third, in using all the means, seek God alone. In and through every outward work focus your attention upon the power of God's Spirit and the merits of God's Son. Nothing short of God can satisfy your soul. Therefore, keep your eye on God in all, through all, and above all. Use all the means as means; as ordained, not for their own sake, but in order to renew your soul in righteousness and true holiness.

22. After you have used any of these means, be careful about how you value yourself, how you congratulate yourself for having done some great thing. This is turning all into poison. If God was there, if God's love flowed into your heart, you have forgotten, as it were, the outward work. You see, you know, you feel that God is all in all. Give God all the praise! Let God "in all things be glorified through Christ Jesus"!

3. THE DUTY OF CONSTANT COMMUNION

Do this in remembrance of me. (Luke 22:19, RSV)

1. I shall show that it is the duty of all Christians to receive the Lord's Supper as often as they can and then answer some objections to this view.

Holy Communion: Gift and Command

2. The first reason for all Christians to receive the Lord's Supper as often as they can is because it is a plain command of Christ. This appears from the words of the text: "Do this in remembrance of me." [The sense of

the command is to do this and "continue in this practice so that you constantly call me to memory."] So here the bread and wine are commanded to be received, in remembrance of his death, to the end of the world.

3. A second reason for this constant practice is because of the benefits we receive. The Lord's Supper is a means of receiving the forgiveness of our past sins and the present strengthening and refreshing of our souls. It confirms the pardon of our sins and enables us to leave them behind. [It is a constant reminder and experience of the new creation.] As our bodies are strengthened by bread and wine, so our souls are nourished by the symbols of Christ's body and blood. This is the food of our souls.

4. Since the sacrament gives us strength to follow Christ and leads us on to perfection, participation in this means of grace should be our normal and constant practice. The earliest Christians received the Lord's Supper every time they gathered for worship on the Lord's Day. [Every Sunday was a day of celebration because it was a joyful reminder of the Resurrection.] The early disciples were obedient to the command of Christ and, as a matter of consequence, experienced the presence of the risen Lord in the eucharist. It would be foolishness for us, then, to turn our backs on the feast which our Lord has prepared for us and in which he has promised to be present.

5. Let this be the standard rule: If you desire to please God, and if you have any love for your own soul, then obey God and participate in this grand channel of grace as often as you can. If time permits, try to prepare yourself properly by self-examination and prayer before you commune. But in any case, the only preparation absolutely necessary is this: First, do you desire to obey God in all things, and second, do you wish to receive all that God has promised?

6. Considering constant communion as a command of God, those who do not communicate as often as they can have no piety. Considering it as a mercy, those who choose not to participate in this means of grace have no wisdom. Our power is in the one rule of our duty. Whatever we can do, we ought to do. Our failure to obey God breaks our bond of union with Christ. But the Lord's Supper is more particularly a divine mercy. It has been given as a means to assist us in the attainment of those blessings that God has prepared for us. Through the eucharist we are offered holiness on earth and everlasting glory in heaven.

7. I ask you then, why do you not accept God's mercy as often as you can? God now offers you untold blessings; why do you refuse them? You have an opportunity of receiving God's mercy now; why do you not receive it?

Common Objections Answered

8. The most common objection to constant communion is that "I am not worthy." Quoting Paul they say, "Those who eat and drink unworthily eat and drink damnation to themselves." Surely you are unworthy to receive any mercy from God. But is that a reason for refusing all mercy? God offers you a pardon for all your sins. You are unworthy of it, that is sure, and God knows it. But since God is pleased to offer it nevertheless, will you not accept it?

9. In this text, however, there is no word about being unworthy to eat and drink. Paul speaks of eating and drinking "unworthily." We are told that this means taking the holy sacrament in such a rude and disorderly way that one was "hungry and another drunken." However unworthy you are to communicate, there is no fear of your communicating in this way.

10. If you fear bringing damnation on yourself by this, you fear where no fear is. Fear not the eating and drinking unworthily. But I will tell you what you should fear! You *should not fear* eating and drinking. *Fear disobeying* your Maker and Redeemer; *fear disobeying God's plain command* and thereby ignoring both God's mercy and authority.

11. A second objection is that no one can *live up to the expectations of a sacramental life.* One cannot pretend to lead so holy a life as constantly communing would obligate one to do. I answer: All that you profess at the Lord's Table you must both profess and keep or you cannot be saved. For you profess nothing there but this, that *you will diligently keep God's commandments.*

12. Consider what you say, therefore, before you say you cannot live up to what is required by constant communion. This is no more than is required of any communicant, indeed, of every one that has a soul to be saved. So to say that you cannot live up to this is neither better nor worse than renouncing Christianity. It is, in effect, renouncing your baptism, wherein you solemnly promised to keep all God's commands and live by the law of love.

13. A third objection is that there is never enough time for proper *preparation before receiving the Lord's Supper.* I answer: All the preparation that is absolutely necessary is contained in those words: "Repent of your past sins and have faith in Christ our Savior." All who are thus prepared may draw near without fear and receive the sacrament to their comfort and strength.

14. If you desire to follow Christ, then you are fit to approach the Lord's Table. If this is not the central purpose of your life, then you are only fit for the table and company of devils. Christ commands you to come, and

to prepare yourself in prayer, if you have time. If you do not have time, however, come! *Do not make reverence for God's command a pretense for breaking it.* Do not rebel against Christ for fear of offending God.

15. A fourth objection to constant communion is that the *repetition will diminish reverence* for the sacrament. Suppose it did. Has God ever told you that when the obeying of a command abates your reverence to it, then you may disobey it? Reverence for the sacrament may be of two sorts: Either that owing to the novelty of the thing or that owing to our faith and to the love and fear of God. Now the former of these is not properly a religious reverence, but purely natural. The constant receiving of the sacrament will, indeed, lessen *this sort of reverence.* But constant communion *will not lessen true religious reverence;* rather, it will *confirm and increase it.*

16. A final objection has to do with *feelings.* "I have communicated constantly so long," some complain, "but I have not found the benefit I expected." This has been the case with many well-meaning persons. It is important to remember, however, that whatever God commands us to do we are to do whether we feel any benefit thereby or not. Undoubtedly we shall find some benefit sooner or later, though perhaps unconsciously. Perhaps we shall be strengthened unawares, made more fit for the service of God, and more constant in it.

17. Surely this should be enough to make us receive this food as often as we can, though we do not presently feel the happy effects of it as some have done. We ourselves may feel as well as understand when God sees best. Only see that you are duly prepared for it, and the more often you come to the Lord's Table, the greater the benefit you will find there.

Summary

18. It has been shown, first, that if we consider the Lord's Supper as a command of Christ, no one can have any pretense to Christian piety who does not receive it as often as possible. Second, if we consider the institution of the sacrament as a mercy to ourselves, no one who does not receive it constantly can have any pretense to Christian prudence. Third, none of the objections commonly brought against constant communion can be any excuse for the earnest disciple who does not, at every opportunity, obey this command and accept this mercy.

19. Unworthiness is no excuse to constant communion, because none of us need to be afraid of being unworthy in Paul's sense of "eating and drinking unworthily."

Not having enough time for preparation can be no excuse since the only preparation absolutely necessary is an open heart willing to receive.

Its repetition abating our reverence is no excuse since he who gave the command, "Do this," nowhere adds, "unless it becomes too familiar or commonplace."

Our failure to feel its effects is no excuse since its benefits are not dependent upon our feelings but upon the free, unmerited grace of God.

20. If those of you who have neglected constant communion on any of these grounds will lay these things to heart, you will, by the grace of God, come to a better mind and never again forsake this means of being drawn into the love of God.

For Thought and Discussion

1. Many forces, traditions, and experiences shape our lives as people of faith. The manner in which we express our faith in word and action is the product of these formative influences. Identify the primary influences (no more than three) that have formed you as a Christian disciple.

2. Wesley talks frequently about the means and end of religion (pp. 36-37; "Means of Grace," paras. 12-14, 19-22). A mother once confessed that inflexibility concerning her daily devotions sometimes got in the way of her dealing in a loving way with her children. Relate two experiences in which means and ends became confused in your own faith journey. From your own point of view, what is the whole purpose of religion?

3. "Without prayer," says Wesley, "you can never grow in grace." See page 37. Why do you pray? When do you usually pray? Formulate two specific resolutions that will make prayer more central in your life, write them out, and act upon them.

4. In Wesley's "Means of Grace," he enumerates several ways by which God teaches us to love. Where do you turn for support, direction, and nurture? Is this resource a thing, a discipline, a friend, a relative, a mentor on the job?

5. The Bible was central to Wesley ("Means of Grace," paras. 8-9). How has the Bible shaped your life? List two passages of scripture that come

immediately to your mind. Reflect upon their significance in your journey.

6. Describe your most memorable celebration of Holy Communion. How did this experience enrich your life, enable you to grow, or sustain your life of faith? Can you identify the point of need to which God responded through this means of grace?

7. In your own words, try to restate Wesley's assertion in "Constant Communion" paragraph 6: "Considering constant communion as a *command of God,* those who do not communicate as often as they can have *no piety.* Considering it as a *mercy,* those who choose not to participate in this means of grace have *no wisdom.*"

8. Wesley lists five common objections to "Constant Communion" in paragraphs 8-17. Which one of these seems to be voiced most frequently today? Is Wesley's response still appropriate? Give one other objection to frequent communion that you have heard. How would you respond to it?

CHAPTER 4
WHAT TO DO

A. Introduction

To serve the present age,
My calling to fulfill;
O may it all my powers engage
To do my Master's will!

In this well-known hymn, Charles Wesley, borrowing images from Matthew Henry's *Commentary* on Leviticus, sings about the life of true discipleship. His description of the Christian life is both powerful and challenging. You recognize the themes. Our primary calling in life is to serve. Christian vocation is a matter of total commitment that engages all our powers. It is ultimately active, not passive; life in Christ is not something we simply receive, it is a relationship to be lived—something we do.

As disciples of Christ, our vocation is to do God's will. Our unique calling is to embody God's vision of a new age for "the present age." Christ calls us, in essence, to be signs of his kingdom in a broken world. The *shalom* he offers—wholeness of life for individuals and the human family—is a gift already given and a goal toward which we strive. It is not simply the absence of war and violence, but the restoration of wholeness and harmony. It involves both our witness and our service. We bear witness to the transforming power of God's love in Christ (the gift of our vocation) and press on toward the goal of our high calling by becoming the servants of all.

To live for *shalom,* to do those things which make for "peace," is never easy in any age. To set out on this road to discipleship is to place your trust in the way of the cross. To do God's will requires that you disarm your heart, become vulnerable, and allow God to change your spirit, your attitudes, and your actions. What we need to rediscover today is a means to sustain and transmit God's vision of a new age and to work for the restoration of well-being, justice, and peace for all of God's children. No three issues could be of greater importance in our time.

WELL-BEING IN A HUNGRY WORLD

Our world is hungry. Nearly forty thousand innocent victims die each day from hunger-related causes. For the most part, hunger is invisible to those of us who live in the comfort of the West. But hungry people are real, and their suffering is real! Blindness to the plight of the poor only perpetuates the dangerous illusion of security in the materialistic and technological gods of our age. Hunger and poverty, however, undermine the security of our global village, strip the world of its most precious human resources, and thereby undermine the well-being of all. The death of any child from malnutrition is ultimately a loss for the entire human family.

Mother Teresa has said that Christ comes to each of us in the distressing disguise of the poor. To our starving brothers and sisters, God declares: "You shall eat your fill and live secure in your land" (Lev. 26:5). That is a part of God's vision that the fiery prophet Amos recalled. He hammered Israel at the height of that nation's economic and political power because some people went hungry while others feasted.

> I hate your religious festivals; I cannot stand them! Stop your noisy songs. Instead, let justice roll down like waters, and righteousness like an everflowing stream (5:21-24).

From the manna of the wilderness to the loaves and fish of the plain, our God is the One who feeds the hungry. The irony today is that for the first time in history we possess the means and only lack the will to eliminate hunger from the globe.

THE RESTORATION OF JUSTICE

Amos saw the vital connection between hunger and justice. Injustice, in all of its forms, is a related issue, which demands our attention. Our world is divided between the "haves" and the "have nots." Abject poverty for many is the price of affluence for the few. A society of justice cannot be built upon the foundation of oppression. And so, Mary, in her Song of Praise, not only proclaims that God "has filled the hungry with good things," but that God has also "scattered the proud with all their plans. God has brought down mighty kings from their thrones, and lifted up the lowly" (Luke 1:51-52, TEV). God's new age is characterized by a radical reversal of place.

In his struggle for justice in racially torn South Africa, Bishop Desmond Tutu has boldly proclaimed that the Christian is either in favor of evil or in favor of good, either on the side of the oppressed or on the side of the oppressor. No true disciple can be neutral. A part of Christian vocation today is our struggle for justice. This struggle is ultimately a quest to free all of God's children, oppressed and oppressor alike.

EMBRACING NONVIOLENCE

Not only is our world hungry and unjust, it is violent. We are all affected by that violence in one way or another.

Self-esteem is destroyed in many of our children—
a violation of our hope for the future.
The threat of nuclear annihilation holds us all in bondage—
a violation of our freedom to live faithfully
in the present.
Nearly 70 wars since 1960 have been fueled by a
massive international arms trade—
a violation of the law of love that restricts us to
the errors of the past.

Our choice today, as Martin Luther King, Jr., prophesied, is not between violence and nonviolence, but between nonviolence and nonexistence. What can we do?

God announced the inbreaking of a new kingdom. Through the prophet Isaiah, God proclaimed a glorious vision:

The great nations will hammer their swords into plows and their spears into pruning knives. Nations will never again lift up swords against one another; neither shall they learn war any more (2:4).

Isaiah asserts that integrity creates peace; that only justice can produce lasting security. The Psalmist echoes the theme: "Steadfast love and faithfulness will meet; justice and peace will embrace each other" (Ps. 85:10, TEV). To be a disciple of the Prince of Peace means daring to hope in the struggle for justice that brings peace. In doing the Word—in living the Vision—we become a presence of healing and reconciliation in our violent world. To do God's will is to model our ministry upon our Lord's example of solidarity with the poor, liberation of the oppressed, and nonviolence in the face of evil.

When you turn to the selections from Wesley in this chapter, you will be struck by the contemporary ring of his words. While the shape of human problems changes, the issues remain perennial. People suffer. The abuse of power and the corrupting influence of greed lead to various forms of human bondage. Violent conflict shatters lives. In the midst of these circumstances, the Methodist people valiantly "offered Christ" in word and deed, witness and service. They distinguished themselves by a style of life that combined living for and in God's vision of *shalom*.

Concern for that vision of well-being, justice, and peace is reflected in the selections which follow. Wesley believed that the decline of Christianity was due in large measure to the failure of Christ's disciples to identify with the poor. Wesley believed that the kingdom of God belonged to the poor. His movement started among them and never lost sight of them during his lifetime. His solidarity with the poor required him to confront the unjust structures of his own society. Not only did he expose injustice wherever he could ferret it out, but he waged peace as the noblest form of Christian service.

All three of the treatises presented here were written by Wesley during the critical decade of the 1770s. They reflect the maturity and wisdom of a man who had confronted tremendous evil and emerged with his optimism in God's grace and the power of love unshaken. In his *Thoughts on the Present Scarcity of Provisions* (January 1773), Wesley attempts to address the issue of hunger in its larger context as a major social problem. Not satisfied with the response of many simply to relieve the symptoms, his concern is to identify the root causes of hunger. His discussion of the problem reveals a consistent understanding of the interconnectedness of life. For good or ill, my decisions and actions influence the lives of other innocent people.

Thoughts Upon Slavery was written in the early months of 1774. The port city of Bristol, one of Methodism's primary bases in the early years of the movement, was heavily dependent upon this lucrative "industry." Wesley knew the dangers of speaking out against this social evil. But he refused to abdicate his calling as an advocate for the oppressed. The constant refrain of his treatise is "justice, mercy, and truth." He had counted the cost and fully expected the vindictive opposition which followed the publication of his volatile pamphlet.

When Wesley wrote his _Seasonable Address to the More Serious Part of the Inhabitants of Great Britain_ (1776), England was locked in a bitter conflict with its prodigal colonies in America. In the treatise, Wesley describes himself as a "Lover of Peace," and in spite of his shifting attitudes with respect to the American grievances, his primary concern was to bring a swift end to the fratricidal war. Indeed, the conflict evoked some of the strongest anti-war statements to come from his pen. We do well to reflect upon his realistic depiction of war and the destructive consequences of violence. Wesley provides a model of nonviolent conflict resolution that stands in direct opposition to standard models of military intervention. Only this Christian alternative can pave the way toward the realization of _shalom_ in our broken world.

B. Wesley Speaks

1. SELECTIONS ON THE INTEGRITY OF FAITHFUL WITNESS AND SERVICE

Faithful Witness

I found [the Societies in Yorkshire] all alive, strong, and vigorous of soul, believing, loving, praising God their Savior, . . . From the beginning they had been taught both the law and the gospel. "God loves you; therefore love and obey him. Christ died for you; therefore die to sin. Christ is risen; therefore rise in the image of God. Christ liveth evermore; therefore live to God, till you live with him in glory." So we preached; and so you believed. This is the scriptural way, the Methodist way, the true way. God grant we may never turn therefrom, to the right hand or to the left.

(In "Of Preaching Christ," 1779)

Let love not visit you as a transient guest, but be the constant temper of your soul. See that your heart be filled at all times, and on all occasions, with real, undissembled benevolence; not to those only that love you, but to every soul of man. Let it pant in your heart; let it sparkle in your eyes; let it shine on all your actions. . . . Every one that is born of a woman has a claim to your good will. You owe this, not to some, but to all.

(In "On Pleasing All Men," 1787)

Do good. Do all the good you can. Let your plenty supply your neighbor's wants; and you will never want something to do. Can you find none that need the necessities of life, that are pinched with cold or hunger; none that have not raiment to put on, or a place . . . to lay their head; none that are wasted with pining sickness; none that are languishing in prison? If you duly considered our Lord's [command] . . . you would no more ask, "What shall I do?"

(In "On Worldly Folly," 1790)

Serving Christ in the Poor

Many years ago, when I was at Oxford, on a cold winter's day, a young maid (one of those we kept at school) called upon me. I said: "You seem half starved. Have you nothing to cover you but that thin linen gown?" She said: "Sir, this is all I have!" I put my hand in my pocket, but found I had scarce any money left, having just paid away what I had. It immediately struck me: "Will thy Master say, 'Well done, good and faithful servant? Thou hast adorned thy walls with the money which might have screened this poor creature from the cold!'"

(In "Advice with Regard to Dress")

At this season we usually distribute coals and bread among the poor of the Society; but I now considered they wanted clothes as well as food. So on this and the four following days I walked through the town and begged two hundred pounds, in order to clothe them that wanted it most.

(In the Journal, dated January 4, 1785. The 81-year-old founder of Methodism left an amazing legacy to his followers through such acts.)

Go and see the poor and sick in their own poor little hovels. Take up your cross, woman! Remember the faith! Jesus went before you and will go with you. Put off the gentlewoman; you bear a higher character.

(In a letter to Miss March, dated 1775)

O that God would enable me once more, before I go hence and am no more seen, to lift up my voice like a trumpet to those who gain and save all they can, but do not give all they can! . . . Many of your brethren, beloved of God, have not food to eat; they have not raiment to put on; they have not a place where to lay their head. And why are they thus distressed? Because you impiously, unjustly, and cruelly detain from them what your Master and theirs lodges in your hand on purpose to supply their wants! See that poor member of Christ, pinched with hunger, shivering with cold, half naked! Meantime you have plenty of this world's goods—of meat, drink, and apparel. In the name of God, what are you doing?

(In "Causes of the Inefficacy of Christianity," 1789)

Exposing Injustice

Here I would beg your serious attention, while I observe that, however extensively pursued, and of long continuance, the African trade [slavery] may be, it is nevertheless iniquitous from first to last. It is the price of blood! It is a trade of blood, and has stained our land with blood! . . . What peace therefore can we expect, while these evils continue? "There can be no peace, saith the Lord." While "the voice of thy brother's blood crieth unto me from the ground," "what hast thou to do with peace?"

(In "A Seasonable Address," 1776)

Unless the divine power has raised you up to be as Athanasius *contra mundum* [Athanasius against the world], I see not how you can go through your glorious enterprise in opposing that execrable villainy [slavery] which is the scandal of religion, of England, and of human nature. . . . O be not weary of well doing! Go on, in the name of God and in the power of his might, till even American slavery (the vilest that ever saw the sun) shall vanish away before it.

Reading this morning a tract wrote by a poor African, I was particularly struck by that circumstance that a man who has a black skin, being wronged or outraged by a white man, can have no redress; it being a "law" in all our colonies that the oath of a black against a white goes for nothing. What villainy is this?

> *(In a letter to William Wilberforce, dated February 24, 1791. Written just a week prior to his death and the last piece of his correspondence, this letter reflects Wesley's lifelong concern for justice and his vigorous opposition to slavery.)*

But may not women, as well as men [exercise their gifts in ministry]? Undoubtedly they may; no, they ought; it is proper, right, and their obligation. Herein there is no difference; "there is neither male nor female in Christ Jesus." Indeed it has long passed for a maxim with many, that "women are only to be seen, not heard." And accordingly many of them are brought up in such a manner as if they were only designed for agreeable playthings! But is this doing honor to the sex? or is it a real kindness to them? No; it is the deepest unkindness; it is horrid cruelty; . . . I know not how any woman of sense and spirit can submit to it. Let all you that have it in your power assert the right which the God of nature has given you. Yield not to that vile bondage any longer! . . . you too are called of God!

> *(In "On Visiting the Sick," 1786. Wesley's outspoken advocacy of women's rights has led some to describe him as one of the greatest "feminist" thinkers of the eighteenth century.)*

Waging Peace

Beware of despising your opponents! Beware of anger and resentment! Return not evil for evil, or railing for railing. . . . Violent methods of redress are not to be used, till all other methods fail. . . . To live peaceably with all men is the earnest desire of your affectionate brother.

> *(In a letter to John Crook, dated August 10, 1776. After having purchased his discharge from the army, Crook became a local preacher on the Isle of Man. Major persecutions quickly ensued, to which Wesley responded with this advice.)*

Prince of universal peace,
　　Destroy the enmity;
Bid our jars and discords cease,
　　Unite us all in thee!
Cruel as wild beasts we are
Till vanquished by the mercy's power.
Men like wolves each other tear.
And their own flesh devour.

But if thou pronounce the word
　　That forms our souls again,

Love and harmony restored
Throughout our earth shall reign;
When thy wondrous love they feel
The human savages are tame;
Ravenous wolves and leopards dwell
And stable with the lamb.

O that now, with pardon blest,
We each might each embrace!
Quietly together rest,
And feed upon thy grace,
Like our sinless parents live!
Great Shepherd, make thy goodness known,
All into thy fold receive,
And keep us ever one!
(In "Short Hymns on Select Passages of
Scripture," 1762)

There is still more horrid reproach to the Christian name, yea, to the name of man, to all reason and humanity. There is war in the world! War between men! War between Christians! I mean, between those that bear the name of Christ, and profess to "walk as he also walked." Now, who can reconcile war, I will not say to religion, but to any degree of reason or common sense?
(In "The Doctrine of Original Sin," 1756)

Who now against each other rise,
The nations of the earth constrain
To follow after peace, and prize
The blessings of thy righteous reign,
The joys of unity to prove,
The paradise of perfect love!
(In "Hymns of Intercession," 1758; and
entitled "For Peace.")

Come let us arise,
And press to the skies;
The summons obey,
My friends, my beloved, and hasten away!
The Master of all
For our service doth call,

And deigns to approve
With smiles of acceptance our labour of love.

His burden who bear,
We alone can declare
How easy his yoke;
While to love and good works we each other provoke,
By word and by deed,
The bodies in need,
The sick to relieve,
And freely as Jesus hath given to give.

Then let us attend
Our heavenly friend
In his members distressed,
By want, or affliction, or sickness oppressed;
The prisoner relieve,
The stranger receive,
Supply all their wants,
And spend and be spent in assisting his saints.
(In "Hymns and Sacred Poems," 1749. Written by
Charles Wesley for his bride.)

2. THOUGHTS ON THE PRESENT SCARCITY OF PROVISIONS

1. Many excellent studies have been published recently concerning the widespread problem of hunger. One expert insists that the current food shortage is due to this particular cause. Another assigns the blame to one or two more. Few seem to be interested, however, in viewing the problem as a whole. No one is addressing the root causes of hunger and the way in which they are interrelated in our society.

The Fact of Hunger

2. First we must ask why thousands of people are starving in every part of our country? The fact I know! I have seen the grim effects of hunger in every part of the land. I have known those who could only afford to have a

meal of scraps once every other day. With my own eyes I have witnessed a woman picking her way through a pile of garbage, hoping to find pieces of stinking fish to carry home for herself and her children.

3. I have seen another gathering the bones which the dogs left in the streets and making broth from them in order to prolong a wretched life! One day I heard a person say:

> I was very faint and so weak I could hardly walk. But my dog, finding nothing at home, went out and brought back a good sort of bone. I took it out of his mouth and made a good dinner!

Many people are subjected to this sort of life in a land flowing, as it were, with milk and honey! While these people suffer, others abound in all the necessities, conveniences, and superfluities of life!

The Causes of Hunger

4. Now why is this? Why are so many starving before our very eyes? An examination of some particular cases will reveal the causes. First of all, the main reason flour is so expensive is because such immense quantities of grain are continually consumed by distilling. Instead of being used for bread, it is used to produce gin. Indeed, a little less than half the wheat produced in the kingdom is consumed every year, not by so harmless a way as throwing it into the sea, but by converting it into deadly poison. This poison destroys not only the strength and life, but also the morals of our nation!

5. Another cause of hunger and poverty is luxury. What can stand against this? Will it not waste and destroy all that human ingenuity can produce? Only look into the kitchens of the rich. When you have observed the amazing waste which is made there, you will no longer wonder why others suffer. Gentlemen cannot maintain their standard of living without increasing their income. So they raise their rents. The farmer, paying a higher rent for his land, must receive a higher price for his produce. And so the wheel runs round.

6. Another reason for our present situation is the enormous burden of taxes. But why are the taxes so high? Because of the national debt. Until the debt is discharged, the taxes must remain high. I have heard that the national expense, seventy years ago, was, in time of peace, three million pounds a year. And now, the bare interest on the public debt amounts to above four million pounds annually! So long as the govern-

ment maintains its current level of expense, those taxes are absolutely necessary.

7. To sum up the whole: Thousands of people are starving to death because they do not have food. This is due to a number of causes, but primary among them are distilling, taxes, and luxury. Here is the evil and the undeniable causes of it. But where is the remedy?

Striking at the Root of the Problem

8. The price of wheat, and therefore of bread, can be reduced by prohibiting distilling. Not only does this industry rob innocent children of the staff of life, it is the bane of health. It destroys strength, and life, and virtue.[8] The repression of luxury would also help the hungry. Whether by laws, by example, or by both [the rich must see that their luxury is purchased at the expense of the poor]. Taxes must be reduced and foolish expenses eliminated in the government in order to help the poor. A million pounds could be saved each year by abolishing useless spending by the Governors of forts or castles.

9. But will this ever be done? I fear not. What good can we expect (suppose the scriptures are true) for such a nation as this, where there is no fear of God. It seems as if God must shortly arise and maintain the cause of justice by divine means. If so, let us fall into the hands of God, and not into the hands of God's faithless children.

3. THOUGHTS UPON SLAVERY

1. [Having defined slavery and summarized its history, and having described the African people and the slave trade to which they have been subjected, it only remains to expose the injustice of this execrable villainy.] The main argument of the oppressors is that slavery is authorized by law. But can human law change the justice of God's created order? Can it turn darkness into light, or evil into good? By no means! Right is right, and wrong is still wrong. There is still an essential difference between justice and injustice, cruelty and mercy. And slavery cannot be reconciled either with mercy or justice!

---

[8]The problems related to the gin industry in Wesley's day are well known. Hogarth's sketches vividly portrayed the misery that overconsumption of alcohol caused for the impoverished masses of the industrial cities. Wesley demonstrated keen insight in his relating of this major social problem to that of hunger.

Exposing Injustice

2. Is it just to inflict the severest evils on those that have done no wrong? Is it right to tear people away from their native home and deprive them of liberty? The Angolan cherishes freedom and possesses it as a natural right as well as any Englishman. Where is the justice in killing innocent, inoffensive people; murdering thousands of them in their own land; many thousands, year after year, on shipboard, and casting them like dung into the sea; and tens of thousands in that cruel slavery to which they are so unjustly reduced? I strike directly at the root of this complicated villainy. I absolutely deny that slavery can be reconciled with any degree of natural justice.

A Merciless Sin

3. Slavery is also utterly inconsistent with mercy. This is too plain to even require proof. Some slave traders have argued that they subject Africans to slavery in order to save them from miserable lives or even death. Was it to save them from death that they knocked out the brains of those they could not bring away? They know their own conscience, if they have any conscience left. To make the matter short: Can they say before God that they ever took a single voyage, or bought a single slave, from this motive? They cannot! They know all too well that the only motive of their actions was to get money, and not to save lives!

Exposing the Argument of Necessity

4. Even though slavery is inconsistent both with mercy and justice, some argue that it is simply necessary. "Damn justice," is their short and plain reply; "slavery is necessary." You stumble from your first step. I deny that any villainy is ever necessary. It is impossible that it should ever be necessary for any reasonable creature to violate all the laws of justice, mercy, and truth. No circumstance can make it necessary for any person to tear apart all the ties of humanity! It can never be necessary for a rational being to sink below a brute! The absurdity of the assumption is so glaring, I wonder how any can fail to see it.

5. For those who argue that slaves are required for the cultivation of new frontiers, my response is plain. It would be better to sink those new lands to the depth of the sea than to develop them at so high a price as the

violation of justice, mercy, and truth. For those who argue for the trade, wealth, and glory of our nation; listen to me. Wealth is not necessary to the glory of any nation; but wisdom, virtue, justice, mercy, generosity, true patriotism, and love of country. Better no trade than trade procured by villainy. It is far better to be penniless than to become rich at the expense of virtue. Honest poverty is of much greater value than riches bought by the tears, and sweat, and blood of our fellow human beings!

Advocacy of the Oppressed

6. How shall we bring an end to this misery? Should we address ourselves to the general public? This would only inflame the world against the guilty, but is not likely to remove the guilt. Should we appeal to the nation? This is also striking too wide and will probably not bring an end to the evil. It is only the oppressors themselves who can end this reign of injustice. And so, I add a few words to those who are more immediately concerned, whether captains, merchants, or planters.

7. May I speak plainly to you? I must! Love constrains me; love to you as well as to those with whom we are concerned. Is there a God? You know there is. Is God just? If so, there must be a state of retribution, a state wherein God rewards people according to their works. What reward will God render you? O think about this carefully, before you drop into eternity! What if God should deal with you, as you have dealt with your African brothers and sisters?

8. Are you a human being? Then you should have a human heart. What is your heart made of? Is there no compassion within you? Do you never feel another's pain? Have you no sympathy, no sense of human misery? When you saw the tear-filled eyes, the heaving breasts, or the bleeding sides and tortured limbs of your fellow human beings, was your heart a stone? Have you degenerated to a brute? When you squeezed the agonizing creatures down in the ship, or when you threw their poor mangled remains into the sea, didn't you feel any guilt? Did not one tear drop from your eye? The great God will surely deal with you and require all of their blood at your hands.

9. But if your heart does relent, though in a small degree, know it is a call from the God of love. And "today if you will hear God's voice, do not harden your heart." Resolve today, God being your helper, to escape for your life. Do not make money your god! Whatever you lose, don't lose your soul. Quit this horrid crime immediately and become an honest

human being. Give liberty to whom liberty is due, that is to every child of God. Away with all whips, all chains, all compulsion! Be gentle toward all people. See that you invariably do unto every one as you would have others do unto you.

4. A SEASONABLE ADDRESS BY A LOVER OF PEACE

1. Who that has any understanding, mercy, and compassion would not do everything possible to prevent war? For who knows, when the sword is once drawn, where it may stop? Who can command it to be put up into its scabbard? It will not obey!

The Victims of War

2. The victims of war not only include the soldier of the field but his beloved wife, an aged parent, a tender child, a dear relative. What can make up for such a loss? What, O! What would the whole world mean if it might be gained? Alas! What a poor trade! But suppose you escape with your life and the lives of those that are near and dear to you. There is another dreadful consequence: plunder and all the evil it entails. O brothers and sisters, can we not abandon war forever?

3. Stop and survey the desolation of war. Behold the weeping and disconsolate widow refusing to be comforted! Her beloved husband is fallen! is fallen! and is no more! See the affectionate parent hanging down his head like the bulrush! Hear the broken language of a mother's heart! "My son! my son! would God I had died in your place! O my son! my son!" This is the real and actual condition of war. While we are biting and devouring one another, these stronger beasts of prey step in and divide the spoil!

4. What is war? Look! Here are some thousands of our brave countrymen gathered together on this plain. They are followed by the most tender and feeling emotions of wives, children, and an innumerable multitude of their thoughtful, humane, and sympathizing countrymen. Then turn your eyes and behold a superior number at a little distance, who only a few years earlier were fellow Englishmen. These are "flesh of their own flesh, and bone of their bone." Likewise they are loved and cared for by wives, and children, and friends.

5. They advance towards each other, prepared with every instrument of death! But what are they going to do? To shoot each other through the head or heart; to stab and butcher each other, and hasten one another (it

is to be feared) into the everlasting burnings. Why so? What harm have they done to one another? Why, none at all. Most of them are entire strangers to one another. But a matter is at dispute relative to the mode of taxation. So these countrymen, children of the same parents, are to murder each other with all possible haste, to prove who is in the right! Now what an argument is this! What a method of proof! What an amazing way to resolve conflict! O, at what a price is the decision made! By the blood and wounds of thousands; the burning of cities; ravaging and laying waste the country!

Resolving Conflict

6. Now, who that seriously considers this tragedy can help lamenting the astonishing lack of wisdom. Are there no wise people among us? Can no one resolve this conflict by any other means? Brother goes to war against brother; and that in the very sight of people who do not know Christ. Surely this is an inexcusable evil! How are the mighty fallen! How is wisdom destroyed! What a flood of folly and madness has broken in upon our civilization!

7. Argument seems lost in the screaming. Confusion of passion and position reign. The satanic dust of prejudice seems to have put out the eyes of our understanding. While we are contending who set the building on fire, and looking with rage and vengeance on the suspected party, the flames are spreading and threaten the entire building. Instead of bringing the water of heartfelt grief and sincere concern, with the helping hand of wisdom, moderation, and love, we consume ourselves in the flames of war.

8. Let us cease contending with each other. Let us avoid unkind and bitter reflection on one another, seeing it can do no real service to the cause we would defend. Let us resolve not to bring combustible matter of this sort to increase the fire. Instead, let us do our utmost to extinguish the blaze. Jesus described the Christian family as the salt of the earth. Exert the seasoning, preserving quality with which you are favored. Bring your adversaries into your loving arms of faith and prayer. Remember them earnestly before the God who loves you both.

9. Let no Christian engage in the controversy in the spirit and temper of the world. Do not bite and devour one another, unless you wish to be consumed with the world. Rather, let your mind be that of the Prophet:

I wish my head were a well of water, and my eyes a fountain of tears, so that I could cry day and night for my people who have been killed (Jer. 9:1, TEV).

There could be no more admirable way of showing our love for our country! We could find no better service!

10. The Bible gives a clear account of the rise and fall of empires. They rose by virtue; they fell by vice. "Righteousness" alone exalts a nation; but "sin is a reproach to any people." And this will always be the case, even to the end of all things. What peace can we expect, therefore, as long as we participate in such evil? As long as we follow this course we are doomed to destroy ourselves. Our acknowledgment of our sin is the first and principal means of restoring the peace we all desire. Reconciliation comes as we accept the friendship of God. If we remember our own sin, and not that of our neighbor, God's power to reconcile will be at work among us. And if the Prince of Peace is with us, who can be against us?

For Thought and Discussion

1. From the hymns quoted in the selections (pp. 58-60), compile a list of the images and words which Wesley uses to envision God's dream for humanity. Where have you encountered this *shalom* or glimpsed the reality of the vision?

2. One of the early Fathers of the church said that theology without action is the theology of demons. Identify those areas within the life of our world today where the church needs to be most active. Is your church faithful in action right now? Are you participating?

3. Wesley believed that affluence was one of the "Causes of the Inefficacy of Christianity" (p. 57). Quickly survey your own budget. How does it correspond to Wesley's principle: gain all you can, save all you can, give all you can?

4. In the quotation from "On Visiting the Sick" (p. 58), Wesley advocates equal rights for women. This was one of many justice issues he championed. Name one other form of injustice you encounter today in your community, in your church, in your home. What actions can you take as a witness for justice and truth?

5. Wesley calls us to be advocates for the oppressed. Consider paragraph 4 of "Thoughts Upon Slavery" very closely. Replace the word *slavery* with a current form of oppression or injustice (e.g., apartheid in South Africa, abortion, exploitation of Central American or South East Asian resources and labor). How does greed influence your decisions about products or people?

6. In the Bishop's Pastoral Letter, *In Defense of Creation,* peacemaking is described as "a sacred calling of the gospel, blessed by God, making us evangelists of *shalom.* Peacemaking is ultimately a spiritual issue: It compels the conversion of minds and hearts." How does this statement compare to Wesley's vision in "A Seasonable Address," paragraphs 6-10? Name one way you have been a peacemaker in your home, at school or on the job, and in your community.

EPILOGUE

God's calling is always an invitation to participate with the family of God in the blessings of salvation. Those who believe are then called into the fellowship of Christ, into peace, into freedom, and into a life of joyful service. Every child of God is called to a particular task, and provided the gifts to fulfill it. Perhaps this study of Christian vocation in the Wesleyan tradition has illuminated an unexplored area in your own pilgrimage with Christ. Perhaps you have awakened a gift, a new relationship, a unique ministry, an exciting area of mission in your community. Remember that Christ is the power and wisdom of God to those who are called.

Together we hope that this is only the beginning of a wonderful adventure. Since Christian vocation is "rooted in the transforming experience of God's grace in Christ Jesus and realized through the power of the Holy Spirit," the dimensions of your life in and with God are boundless. Your true vocation in life is to love as you have been loved by God in Christ. There is no limit to the ways in which that love can be expressed in your life through witness and service. Continue to explore; allow the Living Word to form and transform your life; wait for God in the means that Christ has ordained.

Your vocation in Christ is both a gift and a goal. While intensely personal, it is impotent apart from the community of faith. It is your participation in a glorious drama—the embodiment of God's vision of wholeness for your life and the life of the world. This quest for *shalom* involves much struggle, but is also the source of our greatest hope. And it is only when you risk embracing life's tensions and challenges that your pilgrimage with Christ will become an adventure full of hope. As a people of faith, we are "sure of the things we hope for; we are certain of the things we cannot see." But above all else, Christian vocation is a joyous life of faith which seeks understanding. When lived out in the spirit of Wesley, this journey is one of faith which works by love and leads to holiness of heart and life.

69

The Character of a Methodist[9]

1. Since the name first came into popular use, many have been at a loss to know exactly what it means to be a Methodist. What are the principles and practices that characterize the life of such a disciple? What are the distinguishing marks of this "sect" which is spoken against everywhere? The "Methodists" did not choose this title for themselves; rather it was used originally to ridicule their disciplined life of faith. Even though some may still hate what we are called; perhaps they may learn to love what we are by the grace of God.

2. Methodists are not distinguished by their opinions. We believe that all scripture is inspired by God. We believe that the Bible is the only and sufficient rule both of faith and of practice. We believe Christ to be the eternal, supreme God. But with regard to opinions that do not strike at the root of Christianity, we think and let think.[10]

3. Neither is our religion, or any part of it, to be reduced to the way we talk about God or faith. Our living faith is not to be found in any peculiar way of speaking or any set of uncommon expressions. [Our language can only reflect a small part of the fullness and variety of divine Love.] It is a terrible mistake, therefore, to identify Methodists simply by their words. In fact, we don't want to be characterized by any human symbols, whether they are words, actions, customs, or peculiar traditions.

4. The Methodists, likewise, are not set apart by their emphasis upon any one part of the whole of religion. If you say simply that a Methodist believes "we are saved by faith alone," you do not understand the fullness of the terms. Salvation for the Methodist is holiness of heart and life. And all Methodists affirm that this goal of the Christian life is the consequence of true faith alone. Faith and love, grace and holiness must never

[9] In *The Character of a Methodist,* Wesley sought to describe the noble simplicity of Christian discipleship. Growth in grace and in the knowledge and love of God was the dominant center of his life. Love of God and neighbor was the burning focus of his ministry. "Not as though I had already attained," he noted on the title page of this brief tract, "either were already perfect." Wesley was realistic about the limitations of our human situation. But with God, he would say, all things are possible. One admirer hoped that this treatise would excite some "to walk with greater integrity in the way of the gospel." May it be so.

[10] Wesley draws an important distinction here between the "essentials of the faith" and "opinions" concerning matters of a lesser consequence. As long as the essentials were clear (we have analyzed these as the "hub of belief"), he allowed remarkable liberty with regard to opinion. Wesley was as much opposed to "dogmatism" on the one extreme as he was to "indifferentism" on the other. Here is a healthy and balanced form of doctrinal "pluralism" which makes a unique contribution to the life of the church today.

be separated. The fullness of life in Christ cannot be reduced to either doing no harm, or doing good constantly, or participating in the means of grace. True religion, according to the Methodists is [faith working by love leading to holiness].

5. Who then are the Methodists? Methodists are those disciples of Christ who have "the love of God poured out into their hearts by means of the Holy Spirit, who is God's gift to them" (TEV). They love God "with all their hearts, with all their soul, with all their mind, and with all their strength." God is the joy of their hearts, and the desire of their souls. They constantly cry out: "Whom have I in heaven but you? There is nothing I desire but you! My God and my all! You are the strength of my heart, and my portion for ever!"

6. Methodists are happy in God. Having found salvation through Christ, and forgiveness for all their sins, they cannot help rejoicing. They rejoice now because God has given the gift of a new relationship to them in Christ. Through him they have found peace with God. And they rejoice whenever they look to the future because of their hope in the glory they have been promised in him.

7. They have learned to be content in their life. They know what it means to be humble and how to live with plenty. Everywhere and in all things they are instructed both to be full and to be hungry. They pray without ceasing. Not that they are always in church on their knees, but the language of their hearts is:

> Thou brightness of the eternal glory,
> Unto thee is my heart,
> Though without a voice,
> And my silence speaketh unto thee.

8. This commandment is written upon their hearts: Whoever desires to love God must love neighbor! And so, they love their brothers and sisters in the world as they love themselves. Their hearts are full of love to all humankind. This is their one desire because it is the will of God. Their eye is single. Their one intention is to love as they have been loved.

9. Their obedience to God's will, therefore, is in proportion to God's love, the source from which it flows. Loving God with all their heart, they serve God with all their strength. They present their souls and bodies as living sacrifices, holy and acceptable to God. They entirely and without reserve devote themselves, all they have and all they are, to the glory of god.

10. Not only is this their intention, but they are able to attain to it by the power of God's grace. Their one invariable rule is this: Whatever you

do, in word or in deed, do it all in the name of the Lord Jesus, giving thanks to God through him." Nothing in the world can hinder them from "running the race that is set before them." [This means that some things in life are very clear to them.]

11. They cannot overeat while others go hungry. They cannot "store up riches for themselves here on earth." They cannot waste their money on expensive clothes. They cannot join in or countenance any amusements that are sinful. They cannot speak evil of their neighbors. Love keeps the door of their lips. But whatever is pure, whatever is lovely, whatever is just, they think, and speak, and act, "adorning the gospel of our Lord Jesus Christ in all things."

12. Finally, as they have time, they do good to all people. They feed the hungry; they provide clothing for the needy; they visit the sick; they go to prisons and try to bring light to the lost. Not only do they attend to these physical needs that they see all around them, but they offer Christ to God's children wherever they go. Only God through the grace of our Lord, Jesus Christ, can enable them to do these things.

13. These then are the principles and practices of our "sect." These are the marks of a true Methodist. If you say, "Why, these are only the common fundamental principles of Christianity!" this is the very truth. I know they are no other; and I would to God that both you and all other people knew how we refuse to be distinguished from any other group but by the common principles of our faith. All I teach is the plain, old Christianity, renouncing and detesting all other marks of distinction.

14. Whoever conforms to what I preach (let them be called what they will, for names change nothing in the nature of the thing), is a Christian. That person is a Christian not in name only, but in heart and life. This is what it means to be a Christian and a Methodist:

> To be inwardly and outwardly conformed to the will of God as revealed in the written Word;
> To think, speak, and live according to the method laid down in the revelation of Jesus Christ;
> To be renewed after the image of God, in righteousness and in all true holiness;
> To have the mind that was in Christ, so as to walk even as Christ also walked.

15. By these marks, by these fruits of a living faith, we seek to distinguish ourselves from the unbelieving world. We wish to be disassociated from all those whose minds and lives are not conformed to the

gospel of Christ. But from real Christians, regardless of their denomination, we have never desired to be separate at all. Do you love and serve God? It is enough! I give you the right hand of fellowship.

You, O man or woman of God, think about all these things. If you are already in this way, press on. If you have strayed from the path, thank God for having brought you back. And now, run the race that is set before you, in the royal way of universal love. . . . Keep an even pace, rooted in the faith once delivered to the saints and grounded in love, in true universal love, until you are swallowed up in love for ever and ever.

(In "The Catholic Spirit," 1750)

Let us join ('tis God commands),
Let us join our hearts and hands;
Help to gain our calling's hope,
Build we each the other up.
God his blessings shall dispense,
God shall crown his ordinance,
Meet in his appointed ways,
Nourish us with social grace.

Let us then as brethren love,
Faithfully his gifts improve,
Carry on the earnest strife,
Walk in holiness of life.
Still forget the things behind,
Follow Christ in heart and mind;
Toward the mark unwearied press,
Seize the crown of righteousness!

Plead we thus for faith alone,
Faith which by our works is shown;
God it is who justifies,
Only faith the grace applies,
Active faith that lives within,
Conquers earth, and hell, and sin,
Sanctifies, and makes us whole,
Forms the Saviour in the soul.

Let us for this faith contend,
Sure salvation is its end;
Heaven already is begun,
Everlasting life is won.
Only let us persevere
Till we see our Lord appear;
Never from the rock remove,
Saved by faith which works by love.

(In "Hymns and Sacred Poems," 1740)

Offer up your reflections, resolves, and the entirety of your life to God in some act of recommitment or rededication. The use of Wesley's Service for Covenant Renewal is highly recommended.